P9-DZN-604

THE CARE OF THE AGED

This is a volume in the
Arno Press collection

GROWING OLD

Advisory Editor
Leon Stein

See last pages of this volume
for a complete list of titles

THE CARE OF THE AGED

Edited by

I. M. RUBINOW

ST. JOSEPH'S UNIVERSITY
HV1461.D45 1980
The care of the aged /
STX

3 9353 00096 5937

ARNO PRESS

A New York Times Company
New York • 1980

Editorial Supervision: BRIAN QUINN

———

Reprint Edition 1980 by Arno Press Inc.

Reprinted from a copy in the Library of the University of Illinois

GROWING OLD
ISBN for complete set: 0-405-12813-4
See last pages of this volume for titles.

Manufactured in the United States of America

———

Library of Congress Cataloging in Publication Data

Deutsch Foundation Conference, Chicago University, 1930.
    The care of the aged.

    (Growing old)
    Sponsored by University of Chicago, Graduate School
of Social Service Administration.
    Reprint of the ed. published by University of Chicago
Press, Chicago, which was issued as no. 14 in series:
Social service monographs.
    Includes index.
    1. Old age--Congresses. 2. Old age pensions--United
States--Congresses. 3. Old age assistance--United
States--Congresses. I. Rubinow, Isaac Max, 1875-1936.
II. Chicago. University. Graduate School of Social
Service Administration. III. Title. IV. Series.
V. Series: Social service monographs ; no. 14.
HV1461.D45 1930a   362.6   79-8683
ISBN 0-405-12800-2

THE UNIVERSITY OF CHICAGO
SOCIAL SERVICE MONOGRAPHS

Published in conjunction with the Social Service Review

——————————*Edited by*——————————

THE FACULTY *of the* GRADUATE SCHOOL
OF SOCIAL SERVICE ADMINISTRATION

THE CARE OF THE AGED

THE UNIVERSITY OF CHICAGO PRESS
CHICAGO, ILLINOIS

—

THE BAKER & TAYLOR COMPANY
NEW YORK

THE CAMBRIDGE UNIVERSITY PRESS
LONDON

THE MARUZEN-KABUSHIKI-KAISHA
TOKYO, OSAKA, KYOTO, FUKUOKA, SENDAI

THE COMMERCIAL PRESS, LIMITED
SHANGHAI

Social Service Monographs, Number Fourteen

THE CARE OF THE AGED

PROCEEDINGS OF THE
DEUTSCH FOUNDATION CONFERENCE
1930

Edited by

I. M. RUBINOW, Ph.D.

Director of the Conference

HV
1461
.D45
1980

THE UNIVERSITY OF CHICAGO PRESS
CHICAGO · ILLINOIS

COPYRIGHT 1931 BY THE UNIVERSITY OF CHICAGO
ALL RIGHTS RESERVED. PUBLISHED JUNE 1931

COMPOSED AND PRINTED BY THE UNIVERSITY OF CHICAGO
PRESS, CHICAGO, ILLINOIS, U.S.A.

INTRODUCTORY NOTE

PAUL H. DOUGLAS

Professor of Economics, University of Chicago

This volume, which embodies the proceedings of a conference on the problems of old age that was held at the University of Chicago under the auspices of the Graduate School of Social Service[1] during the month of March, 1930, should prove of distinct value in clarifying the public mind about the precise steps which it is advisable for society to take.

The problem of old age is steadily becoming more important as the public health movement and the reduction of immigration increase the relative proportion of the total population which is formed by those past the ages of fifty and sixty-five. Not only are the relative numbers of the aged increasing, however, but they are also finding it more difficult to obtain gainful employment. This is largely due to the decline of agriculture and the rise of urban industry, since this means a transition from a society where an old man can work on his home farm to the limit of his powers to a society where men who fall below given levels of efficiency tend not to be permitted to exercise such efficiency as they possess. There is some evidence, moreover, that within the last decade, it has become more difficult for old men to find employment within the field of urban industry itself. This is not so much due to a heartless policy on the part of corporations of discharging older employees, as to the fact that if the older worker once loses his position because of illness, a reduction in the size of the working force, etc., he finds it far more difficult than would a younger man to obtain employment elsewhere. For while many businesses will hold on to their own older workers as long as possible, they tend to be very reluctant to hire new workers who are in the advanced age groups. For these older workers have less capacity for manual tasks, have higher accident rates, are subject to higher group insur-

[1] The School of Social Service provided for this Conference on the special Samuel Deutsch Foundation, which was set up in the School to be used, in part, for undertakings of this kind. The School is also under obligation to this Foundation for providing for publication of the Conference proceedings.

ance premiums, and may impose a moral burden upon the employers to care for them when they come to the age of retirement.

From all of these causes, therefore, there probably tends to be an increasing number of old people in our society who are unable to maintain themselves out of current earnings. Nor are the earnings of unskilled and semi-skilled sufficient to permit their laying aside any appreciable savings for old age. Despite the recent rise of real wages, the average starting rate for unskilled labor on July 1, 1930, was only 43.1 cents an hour. If these unskilled were to work therefore for ten hours a day and 306 days in a year, their maximum yearly earnings would be only $1,315. But this would in turn be subject to deductions for shorter hours, broken time, complete unemployment, and sickness. It is indeed doubtful whether the average annual earnings of the unskilled are greatly in excess of $1,000 a year. Dr. Leila Houghteling, in her study of the earnings of unskilled workers in Chicago, found that of a group, who were quite steadily employed, 69 per cent did not earn enough to maintain those who were actually dependent upon them on the scale which the charitable organizations of Chicago used for relief cases. Even when all other sources of family income were taken into consideration, there were still 45 per cent of the families whose total incomes fell below the minimum set for relief.

When to insufficient earnings are added the disasters which so frequently sweep upon families in the shape of serious accidents, prolonged unemployment, protracted illnesses, and death, it becomes apparent that a large section of our population finds it virtually impossible to build up a stake for old age.

The two chief types of social protection which at present exist for the aged are: (1) public poor relief which generally takes the form of the poorhouse and (2) the voluntary pension plans of private employers. The humiliation attendant upon the first deters large numbers from applying for assistance who are in dire need, while it is, in addition, as Miss Parker's paper shows, an extremely expensive method of caring for the indigent. Private pension plans are necessarily limited in scope since they do not protect widows and spinsters who are not attached to any male and can in the nature of the case include only those who have been employed for a long period of time with a particular company. Furthermore since these pensions are regarded by the courts as gratuities rather than as deferred wages, it is always possible for the companies, if they find the expense of the system to be onerous, to alter the terms in favor of themselves. The result is that the workers or pensioners cannot be certain that they will obtain the provisional benefits. Since most of the private pension plans are actuarially unsound and if carried through will cost industry much more than was originally believed, it can be seen that this is a very shaky reed for the minority under such plans to lean upon for protection.

The very able papers which are contained in this volume seem to me to point toward a threefold line of attack upon the problem: (1) an attempt by industry and society to place the older workers as far as possible in positions where they can function effectively, (2) the establishment of state old age pensions to provide financial aid for the aged poor in their own homes, (3) the development of adequate social work for the aged which will provide not only for the services of trained social workers but also for the hospitalization of the ill and disabled, and competent psychiatric care for those needing such attention.

Industry and society for example cannot continue to give the preference to young people in filling all of the manual positions. For the proportion of the aged in our population is steadily increasing and the proportion of those in the 20–40-year age group steadily diminishing. Professor Warren S. Thompson indeed predicts that by 1975 those over 50 years of age will form no less than 26 per cent of the total population. Under such circumstances, industry cannot afford to neglect the services of this group and will not indeed be able to find a sufficient number of young people to man its ranks. There is need therefore for careful work upon the part of industry and of a public employment service (if such an adequate organization is ever effected) to determine the precise jobs upon which the older men can be employed with little loss of efficiency. When this is done, the older workers can be transferred to these jobs and in some cases be retrained for them.

State old age pensions are another link in the chain of protection. The older state laws which merely permitted counties to pay out such pensions have been demonstrated to be comparatively ineffective because of the reluctance of the counties to impose upon themselves added financial burdens. The second type of law, namely, the permissive act with state aid, and of which Wisconsin and Minnesota are the two most prominent examples, has also demonstrated its comparative inferiority in getting the counties to take affirmative action. The most desirable type of law is therefore that which has recently been passed by California, Massachusetts, New York, and Delaware, namely, a measure which is mandatory upon the counties to put into effect but the expense of which is borne by the state as well as the county. In this way the expense is distributed over a wider area than the county itself so that the wealthier counties may help to bear the burdens of the poorer. At the same time, however, the counties are given an incentive to refrain from excessive expenditure since if this occurs, they will have to pay part of the cost. The state, because of its grants will in turn be enabled to lay down certain minimum standards of efficiency and to exercise general supervision over the administration of the act.

The more recent acts and the bills which are now pending in a number of legislatures indicate that for a considerable period of time the pensionable age will be 70 years. The American people seem moreover to have come to the opinion that the pensions should not be automatic or universal, but should be paid only to those: (1) whose private income is insufficient to maintain them upon a minimum scale, and (2) whose children or other near relatives are unable to support them.

By these means, family responsibility is maintained and the relief given only to those who need it. The pensions from the government are generally limited to $30.00 a month as a maximum (although New York fixes no definite limit) with the provision that the amount of the state pension diminishes proportionately as the private income of the pensioner increases. Some bills wisely provide that a person may have a certain minimum amount of income before any deduction is made from the government pension. It is also interesting to note that many of the laws are giving to the administrative authorities a considerable amount of discretion within these limits.

Although the present laws are non-contributory, it is quite possible that many of them may ultimately be placed on a contributory basis. For it would be impracticable in the beginning to pass a purely contributory law since this would disbar those already aged who would not have had the opportunity of making such contributions. If the age of eligibility were reduced to 65 years, it is possible that this added expense might be met by contributions from the employed themselves or from employees and employers together.

There is a third feature of a balanced social program for old age, namely, the development of adequate social work. It is to be hoped that ultimately every county of proper size shall have a welfare department which will have, as one of its divisions, the care of the aged. If these divisions can be manned by trained social workers, appointed under civil service provisions with the advice of experts, we can have the aged supervised by competent persons. Certainly monetary grants are not enough. The aged need advice and assistance to protect them from exploitation by relatives or by those with whom they are boarding, to prevent them from wasting their own pensions, and to furnish them with the proper medical care and attention. Many of the present poorhouses will moreover be transformed into specialized homes for the ill, the infirm, and the psychopathic aged with the result that some of the old can be sent to institutions which are adapted to their particular needs.

A final question may be raised as to what can be done for those who because of their age find it difficult, if not impossible, to obtain employment but who are not sufficiently old to qualify under the old age pension acts. An adequate system of unemployment insurance would protect many of these. There necessarily would be some however who could not qualify because of not having been employed during the preceding year or years for the minimum period of time which any properly drafted unemployment insurance law would require. These could in part be assisted to find work for which they were suited by an adequate public employment system but there would be a residue which would still have to be cared for by public or private charity. At the very worst therefore their plight will be no worse than it is now. It would in fact probably be better since the private charities could relieve them more adequately once the burden of advanced old age were lifted from them. No system of social welfare can however in itself solve all the problems of industrial old age and it is better to leave this residual to the care of private charity than to weaken the old age pension and unemployment insurance laws by greatly lowering the requirements concerning the minimum age of eligibility and the minimum length of former employment.

I feel that we owe a very real debt to Dean Edith Abbott and Professor Sophonisba Breckinridge who originally conceived the idea of this Conference and who did the initial planning, to those who contributed papers and participated in the discussion, and especially to Dr. I. M. Rubinow who has long been recognized as the foremost American authority on social insurance and who, more than anyone else, is responsible for the success of this Conference.

TABLE OF CONTENTS

THE MODERN PROBLEM OF THE CARE OF THE AGED

I. M. RUBINOW

Cincinnati, Ohio

This conference has been called together for a very definite purpose, to consider from all possible angles the question of proper care of the aged. This is one of the unusual gatherings to which those who are responsible for it need offer no apologies for the small attendance, which is in accordance with the predetermined plans. The purpose of the conference is not so much propaganda (though I for one do not for a moment subscribe to the assumed and often not altogether honest condemnation of all propaganda). In an age when high-power salesmanship has become the main motive force of economic growth and its principles have even penetrated the highest institutions of scientific, ethical, or religious teaching, it is a little naïve to pretend to make faces at propaganda. In social progress, it has its place, but if it is to be a constructive force it must be based upon knowledge, understanding, and a constructive social program. If out of this conference, therefore, there should develop any material for wholesome propaganda, I for one shall have no occasion to regret it, but what the program is to be shall be determined by the collective wisdom and experience of this small group of experts.

It may be only the evidence of a pernicious and irradicable habit, but I cannot help approaching any social problem in terms of quantitative relationships, or at least with an effort toward quantitative measurement. We are, as we are told every day, the richest people in the world, and this period we live in (disregarding for a moment the blizzard of last November and its inevitable but transitory consequences) is the richest period in our history. We are, so to speak, literally wallowing in wealth. It is estimated to equal from 350 billion to perhaps 400 billion dollars, considerably over $3,000 per person. Our annual income, as computed by a reliable statistician, is stated to be over 90 billion dollars, or nearly $800 per capita. If we are to compute these figures on a basis of the so-called standard family of five, or even if we are to be more modern and assume a family of four, an average wealth of $12,000 with an annual income of over $3,000 offers a very solid foundation for national prosperity. Nor need it be assumed for a moment that we have already reached the pinnacle of this economic progress. We need only remember Professor Douglas' estimate of an average unemployment rate of at least 10 per cent, or Stewart Chase's eloquent description of the numerous channels of economic waste even in our efficient economic system. Surely at least we in America are not so greatly in need of a five-year plan of enforced starvation in order to create the necessary supply of capital. The rapid increase of national wealth in face of conspicuous waste is sufficient evidence that we are capable of producing a continuous surplus. We are, indeed, perhaps for the first time in the history of the world, in the position to afford certainly everything we need, if not perhaps everything we may want.

On the whole, as a people we have taken advantage of this economic prosperity, nor have we reached the point of satiety, the point where (no matter what a few philosophic or a few aesthetic individuals might feel) as a people we are ready to say "enough." Though the vast majority of us belong to the wage working class, whether it be of the horny-handed or of the white-collar variety, all of us, at least all the native-born among us, aspire and hope, sooner or later, to enter the great middle class, and those of us who have lost that hope for themselves make their psychologic adjustment by transferring that hope to their children. And the American middle class standard, the ideal if not the real standard as yet, has a family income of approximately $7,500 per annum. So we may expect to go on until we more than double our national income and considerably smooth out the curve of distribution before we would be ready to call a halt.

But already, as it is, on the whole we live comfortably, almost luxuriously, or at least those do whom we are by silent consent including among us. We work shorter hours and fewer days a year. Within comparatively few years we have acquired a summer vacation habit, and are beginning to learn the advantages of a winter vacation as well. We laughed at the English week-end habit until, with our usual love of exaggeration, we've got it worse than our English cousins.

We have learned the gospel of outdoor life, from the multimillionaire down to the Ford tramp. As was recently pointed out by a prominent European economist, the most striking economic tendency of the post-war period was the shifting of emphasis from consumption of necessaries to the consumption of luxuries. The three great staples of food, clothing, and shelter claim a rapidly decreasing proportion of our nationally important expenditures. There is a good deal of evidence that we eat less food. No evidence at all is necessary that we wear less clothing, and we seem to be quite willing to be satisfied with less shelter, at least quantitatively, but we have created innumerable demands for articles of luxury. Our whole economy and psychology has changed from that of pain to pleasure. Surely in economic theory we have stopped paying any attention to the distinction between productive and non-productive consumption.

Given this new economic setting, an entirely new approach is made possible to any problem that confronts us. We need not spin economic utopias as to what might be if, and be satisfied with that sort of purely psychologic compensation. We can, on the contrary, proceed in a businesslike way to study the problem and formulate the necessary solution, leaving the answer to the final question as to how much it is going to cost almost as a simple problem in arithmetic.

The specific problem that this conference has been called upon to survey is the problem of care of the aged. Under any form of social organization, the power of production is necessarily limited to a certain though varying percentage of the population. The power of consumption, on the other hand, is not. It was perhaps one of the naïve evidences of primitive socialism when it based its claims upon a principle that every worker is entitled to the full product of his labor. The productive part of humanity always carried upon its shoulders the burden of the non-productive consumer. The extent to which any particular effort or any particular social national group would carry and provide for non-productive consumers, the scale of this provision can serve as useful measuring rods of national prosperity.

Roughly speaking, our non-productive population may be divided into two groups which perhaps, for want of better terms, might be designated as the normal and abnormal unproductive consumers. The abnormal, non-productive consumers consist of those who are thrown out of the productive process or have never been able to enter it, because of some physical or mental or social abnormality. They are the sick, whether permanently or temporarily so, the mentally deficient, or mentally abnormal, the criminal. That these classes must be provided for is generally admitted, and they are being provided for, albeit not with uniform generosity. We take this provision for granted, forgetting sometimes that even that is a comparatively new aspect of social organization, though even now occasionally atavistic argument is heard that it would be cheaper to eliminate entirely the imbecile or idiot or criminal, or even incurable, than to carry them as a social burden. We are rich enough to recognize the necessity for hospitals, insane asylums, institutions for the feeble-minded, and penitentiaries. We may, if we wish, point to the care of this part of the population as evidence of pure altruism.

There are, however, at least two groups of non-productive consumers who do not come within this classification and who need no appeal to altruistic feelings to claim for themselves a proper share of the national income. In caring for the children and for the aged, we need no exercise of any abstract altruism. We provide for our children because they are the only means of immortality. They are at least our own personalities projected into the future. Nothing is more certain than the fact that we have been children ourselves, and it is almost equally certain, and it is becoming more so with the present standards of health and longevity, that we can't forever remain young and energetic and productive. The aged are not a class. They are a stage of our own lives.

To a very large extent all our life has been tuned up to the care of our children. More and more are the needs of the young studied and provided for in our national as well as in our individual family budgets. It might be a very interesting problem in social psychology to study the reason of the striking neglect of the non-productive period of each and every life at the other end, the purely accidental and haphazard way in which the problem of the aged has been met until today, but one must not allow himself to wander away from the practical problem before us into the fields of speculative psychology. For the present we may be satisfied with the fact that the day seems finally to have come when we are willing at least to consider seriously what we can do for the aged, which, in the final analysis, becomes a very personal problem of what we can do for ourselves when we finally pass into that group.

Who are the old? What does the term mean anyway? Relative terms are much more easily defined than absolute ones. We know who are the older and oldest, but the old are not so readily circumscribed. When we begin to study them in earnest, we find the multitude of groupings present a multitude of problems, and require an even more complicated multitude of measures. It is with this point of view that the present group has been called together, and if the conference accomplishes nothing more than to present constructive evidence of this complexity of problems involved, it will have amply justified itself.

What is old age? It is that stage of life which normally precedes its final dissolution, unless death is superimposed prematurely, whether it be through accident or disease. It is a stage usually characterized by gradual and irreparable failing of all faculties. It is a matter of common knowledge that this stage strikes different individuals at different chronological ages. This gradual process of deterioration does not affect all faculties uniformly and simultaneously. Usually (though there are many exceptions to the rule), physical powers decline long before mental capacities, and one may add, productive powers decline long before powers of consumption. Somehow or other, this consumer's demand must be met. It may be suggested that it can be met out of past accumulations, but the economist knows that by far the largest part of consumers' demand is met out of concurrent and not accumulated wealth.

The first quantitative consideration to be kept in mind is the fact that the proportion of population belonging to this non-productive group is gradually and fairly rapidly increasing. It is increasing because at the other end of human span, there is a rapid decrease, a declining birth-rate. It is increasing because modern medicine and hygiene are reducing the mortality during the productive years. Those are essentially problems in vital statistics, but in addition to them there is an increase in non-productive old age which is due to rapid reorganization of modern industry. The problem of the increasingly rapid superannuation in industry is, therefore, one of the fundamental problems that must be studied at this conference. There may be some technical aspects to this problem, perhaps the effect of exhaustion through the excessive intensity of our productive processes; but perhaps even more important is the economic factor of age limitation in industry, primarily due to competitive conditions under which a great deal of fair productive capacity must be thrown out. The aged may be able to continue to walk around a golf field long after they are forced to give up any ambition of engaging in sprinting races. The extent of this process, the effect upon millions of people, is a grave problem that deserves of much more careful study than has been given to it heretofore.

It is because of this new setting that the problem of what to do with our aged is acquiring such large proportions. Before the advent of the modern industrial era, the problem was largely an individual problem for each family group to carry and care for. Between the time, for instance, that the peasant had to give up all participation in the work of the patriarchal family group and the time of his death the period probably wasn't a very long one. The modern problem of the aged takes in at one end the fairly vigorous man whose graying temples indicate that he may be losing his pep, and on the other the helpless bedridden invalid, for whom perhaps a complicated apparatus of continuous nursing and medical care is necessary. Surely no one formula will meet the needs of all the sub-groupings in this very large class. Perhaps one need not be surprised that where the problem is gravest, it is also comparatively simple. It is in the twilight zones of social problems that theoretical difficulties arise and theoretical differences necessarily occur.

Thus the problem of proper care of the senile, whether physically or mentally, or both, the problem of the disabled through rheumatism, partial paralysis, or other physical diseases is to a large extent and may remain so a problem of proper institutionalization. The bald statement so frequently made that with some specific economic measure such as old age pensions, the closure of all old folks' homes may be rapidly achieved is perhaps as careless and has been perhaps as damaging to the movement as similar promises that in a short time we could dispense with all child-caring institutions. If we are really concerned with making the lives of all the old people as happy as possible, then the problems arising out of proper organization of institutions for the aged remain a permanent problem to which careful attention must be given. And where is there, after all, the vigorous, mature man or woman who can be absolutely certain he may not face such a condition himself? Nor is it the problem simply of proper care. Medical science has hardly begun to make a scientific study of the medical problems of old age out of which may come not only a prolongation of the span of human life, but also a more satisfactory final chapter.

With all that, this group represents only a small minority, which, with some progress in medical science, we may reasonably expect will grow even smaller. The greater bulk of our aged population consists of those who may have to be eliminated out of the productive process but may retain for many years the possibilities of a satisfactory, even happy existence. What provisions exist for them? May I venture a classification of present methods of dealing with old age into the following five groups:

1. There is the exceptional person whose earning capacity remains unimpaired or little impaired. Economically it means that one may avoid old age altogether. Perhaps some startling medical discoveries may largely increase this class. Perhaps, also, a new adjustment of industry to the needs of this class may prove less wasteful, less contrary to modern industrial efficiency than we are ready to admit at present. The prevalence of a large proportion of old folks in government service has always been a subject of ready wit, and yet it offers at least a hint of a possibility of some system of utilizing productive capacity which may be both cheaper and more satisfying than complete elimination with corresponding support. There opens a wide vista both for medical and economic research.

2. There is the retired old age resting on its economic laurels, or drawing upon the savings of a lifetime, a situation undoubtedly more common in this country than in any other, and yet perhaps not quite as common as assumed by some. A recent investigation of this problem by a well-known private organization has summed up

in a conclusion by a phrase which has become fairly famous, "Men in this country stand a better chance of being worth $10,000 or more between sixty-five and seventy-five than of being destitute." There are at least half a dozen ways the very figures of investigation could be qualified, in fact, qualified to such an extent as almost to qualify the entire statement as a thinly disguised and deliberate misrepresentation. But even assuming the accuracy of the statement it only limits and doesn't eliminate the problem of the destitute. To the destitute it is small satisfaction that there are others who are not. And not to the destitute only—to our economic society this limitation is a challenge and even more than a challenge. It is an indictment that out of this enormous accumulation of surplus wealth everybody could not be given the minimum which some people are lucky enough to possess.

3. A very extensive method of meeting the old age problems still remains within the power of the family group. In fact, this is frequently put forth as the only normal ethical and socially desirable method of handling the problem of the aged, so much so that any suggestions as to broad social policy for many years were rejected by serious students on the ground that it might interfere with this more ethical method of family provision. The point of view is based upon disregard of all modern changes, not only in the biological makeup of the family, but also of the social relationships within the family group. What are these changes? To begin with, the concept of a family, at least as a unit of economic responsibility, has been considerably narrowed down practically to children only. With the dispersion of families throughout the country, even siblings retain only a very slight moral and of course no legal responsibility, a striking change from the standards which prevailed comparatively few years ago. Second, a certain proportion of the aged have never married, according to the investigation of the Civic Federation, some 6 per cent. Another 12 per cent, though married, have never had any children. Another 13 per cent have only one child, and some 15 per cent two children. How different from the state of affairs when families ran into from a half-dozen to a dozen children. The problem of the support of an aged parent or two is one thing, when there are a dozen children among whom to distribute the burden,

and quite a different thing when it falls upon one or two. Less than half of the old men interviewed had more than two children to depend upon. Thus, the question of family solidarity as a matter of meeting the problem of old age resolves itself into a great many other questions as to the age, health, and earning capacity of these children, and also their own family obligations. With all these limitations, there must be a very happy concurrence of a great many favorable factors to make the support of aged parents by children a possibility which should not react in a very harmful way upon the younger family groups. Forcing this responsibility upon children even if such forcing be a much easier matter than it really is may thus result in a very complex series of antisocial consequences. That it is a happy, economic, and perhaps an emotional solution in a certain number of cases need not be gainsaid. Of course, we lack the necessary information to say how often the situation is happy economically, and it is even more difficult to determine how frequent emotional resistance may be in such cases. The investigator of the National Civic Federation, for instance, arrives at the conclusion that in 60 per cent of the cases children are able to give full support; in 28 per cent of cases no support; and in only 12 per cent of cases a varying degree of support. The very percentages raise a very serious doubt how far the children would agree with the statistician. Moreover, ability to support doesn't always mean willingness to do so, and the enforcement of such obligation by law hardly promises a happy solution of the problem.

When we leave the three groups described in the foregoing, those who continue supporting themselves, those who have saved up enough to retire, and those who may be supported by their children, we are confronted with the obvious need of some form of public support.

4. There is the group to whom the fourth method available at present is applied, namely, that of public or private charity. Under our present American conditions, this is an important aspect of the problem which should receive due consideration from this conference. This method of voluntary aid, call it charity, philanthropy, or relief, may be and is applied either through public or private agencies. It may be given in the form of institutional care because such care is organized,

or perhaps because no other form of relief is available, or it may be given in a form of outdoor relief, whether public or private. Accurate figures, statistical data, as to the extent to which this method is in use are available for institutions but hardly for outdoor relief. Federal statistics, as well as the splendid recent studies of the United States Bureau of Labor, have given us a great deal of information both as to the quality and quantity of our homes for the aged. Not all the private institutions are as luxurious as some. Not all the public poorhouses, almshouses, or county homes are quite as gruesome as others; but except the comparatively small percentage of those for whom institutional care is necessary, institutionalization of able-bodied aged is frequently unnecessary, cruel, and not infrequently unnecessarily expensive. The psychologic effects of life in these concentration camps for the aged should offer a most interesting subject of investigation, but even without it, in a purely empirical way, every social worker is familiar with the stubborn resistance of most old folks against commitment to an institution.

5. To proceed with the analysis, a fifth group is represented by the various retirement or superannuation schemes. The aspects of superannuation, the requirements of industrial efficiency, and to some extent the humanitarian consideration for the interests of the workers are responsible for a fairly large number of private industrial pension funds. On the whole, they represent a wholesome tendency, even though they always present the danger of being utilized as powerful weapons in the economic struggle between capital and labor, which explains the frequently encountered and at first sight almost incomprehensibly bitter attitude of labor organizations to such schemes. The most emphatic argument brought forth against them is that they may be used as a method of tying up the individual wage worker to a specific industry or employer, and yet by itself, if taken out of the present economic setting, such endeavor on the part of industry to stabilize employment and reduce the labor turnover is, of course, a perfectly healthy one. Under any form of organization, such competitive efforts between employers to attract labor should prove conducive to industrial efficiency as well as contentment. It is quite another matter when these pension funds are used as a club, particularly so when according to our legal concepts they remain

pure gratuities to be granted or taken away at will. Here, again, a large number of very complex problems arise which deserve a most careful consideration, study, and appraisal.

But whatever our verdict may be in regard to these industrial pension funds, the important fact is that as yet only a few have been organized and cover a very small proportion of our wage working masses; that they do not show any tendency toward rapid increase; that they are becoming more and more expensive, and many of them are in danger of being abandoned—in other words, unless they are made a part of a system protected by law, many of them are in danger of becoming promises unfulfilled.

If all the five million men and women over sixty-five years of age could be found distributed among these five groups, that is, either still working or living on their savings, or cheerfully supported by their children in comfort, or taken care of by private pension funds, or maintained in institutions or by satisfactory grants of public or private outdoor relief systems, there still would be a problem, but perhaps not a very pressing one. There still would remain the problem of depopulation of the old folks' homes, at least so far as the fairly healthy inmates are concerned. There still would be a problem whether the stigma of charity and relief should justly be applied to individuals who, after some forty or fifty years of useful economic activity, find themselves without means of earning a living. But the situation is even more complicated than this. When all these five classes can be carefully accounted for, a residuum would still remain —the thousands or perhaps hundreds of thousands of old men and women who have no definite or satisfactory economic basis of existence. There are those who are struggling to earn a pittance, though the employment of old, decrepit, sickly individuals is a disgrace to our civilization, when other hundreds of thousands of able-bodied women and men are looking for work. There are those who eke out a living by begging between short periods of irregular employment. There are those who crowd the squalid poorhouses. There are those whom the children are forced to support and do it grudgingly, thus introducing an element of irritation and discord in hundreds of thousands of families. It is this residuum that constitutes a pressing problem demanding an immediate solution. How big this residuum is we can only guess at present. There are some indications, of course, as to its extent. It is significant, for instance, that even the optimistic report of the National Civic Federation admits that 25 per cent of men and 34 per cent of women over sixty-five years of age own no property at all. It is significant that 40 per cent have no income from work, and that some 17 per cent have neither property nor income. It is significant that over 25 per cent have been found totally unable to do any work, and another 30 per cent able to do only light work, which, added to the disqualification for age, makes them practically unavailable for industry. It is significant that in that investigation outside of the institutions for the aged, only 1½ per cent were supported by public or private charity, and that 40 per cent were assisted primarily by children and to some extent by other relatives and friends. A statistical picture of this character might cause no wonder and perhaps call for no immediate action in impoverished Russia, but it doesn't seem to harmonize very well with the glorious picture of American prosperity.

Must the solution of this problem, must our attitude to the needs of the aged (and the aged after all are only ourselves, only a decade or two or three later) be left to chance, to luck, or to individual philanthropic motive? Is that the most efficient way in which our highly organized society can face a problem of such magnitude and importance? Even if there were no precedents to go by, no examples to follow, even then one might point at this problem as a challenge as to American inventiveness and ingenuity. But as a matter of fact there really is no great need for exercise of this ingenuity or inventiveness, for the problem is not new and solutions have been worked out. They have been applied some forty or fifty years ago, first in one country and another, until at present there practically is not a single industrial country in which there isn't some definite governmental established system of provision for the needy aged. One might say that the problem for us to consider is not what to do, but perhaps what best method to choose from the many available, and how to overcome the stubborn resistance to applying the results of world-wide experience. Even upon that point of view there are already important precedents available. With the same degree of stubbornness they have resisted for many years the application of the principles of workmen's compensation, and I wonder whether any suggestion to abolish compensation and to return to the old system could at this time command the support of even 1 per cent of our population.

European experience can point to two definite methods of a state-wide and a statesmanlike solution of old age—the method of old age pensions and the method of compulsory old age insurance. Undoubtedly, these two methods will be given very careful consideration during the conference. Undoubtedly, adherence of either one of the two methods to the exclusion of the other will be heard. If the conference can arrive at a definite decision in the choice between the two methods, it will have made a very valuable contribution. Perhaps, as I hope personally, that decision may be that there is no fundamental contradiction between the two methods at all; that as European experience has demonstrated, one method does not exclude the other; that perhaps they both might be established simultaneously, or one gradually merge into the other, or the method of old age pensions introduced because of its immediate advantages while more time is taken to elaborate a compulsory system of old age insurance. Whether the fund out of which the aged are supported in a respectable and ample manner is to be collected out of small contributions from millions of insured, or taken out of the available funds of the government, which again must collect them from the people by a system of taxation, is after all substantially a question of procedure, of method but not of principle. The principle involved is that there shall be a planned, organized system based upon a recognition of a responsibility of the majority who can work and earn toward those who did work and earn, but in the natural course of human events have lost that power. Even as children represent our own past, so do the aged represent our own future. Specific provision for the aged is, therefore, not a piece of economic magic. It isn't even an example of that much derided tendency toward paternalism. It is an expression of the same common sense which individually teaches us personal saving where such saving is possible. In its social application, it is only common sense that the principle of a decent and comfortable old age, in its importance for the well-being of society, should take precedence even over the principle of a second car for every American family, or a victrola or a radio in every American home.

This, in brief, is an outline of the problems that this conference is called upon to consider. May I express the hope that out of these two days of deliberation will come a practical program, at least for the city and the state in which we have come together?

SUPERANNUATION IN INDUSTRY

PERRY A. FELLOWS

City Engineer, Detroit Michigan; Vice-President, Society of Industrial Engineers

Few words in the English language flash more vivid pictures across our consciousness than does the word "industry." There was a time when its mention recalled the wholesome, healthful, happy activities of the individual who busied himself at appropriate tasks which he was always able to find; who wasted no part of his valuable hours in daydreaming nor lost his way while wandering through Elysian fields of happy-go-lucky idleness. It brought to mind the farmer, awake at break of day, doing the morning's milking and a dozen other minor chores before the call for breakfast, so that he might have the unclipped day for the duties the changing seasons might bestow upon him. It brought to mind the burly blacksmith who, when there were no horses waiting to be shod, seized that opportunity to hammer bits of iron and steel into useful tools or fashioned at his forge the innumerable little gadgets that found their place of usefulness in the home or shop. These pictures and others of their kind have faded now, and another takes their place.

The later picture is one painted in masses of color with the somber shades predominating. Sketches of individuals give way to impressionistic daubs that have no character and an uncertain value. We see the blazing furnaces and the belching stacks. We hear the clash of metals and the throb of engines, the whir of wheels, and the ceaseless swish and swirl of the endless belts. We lose sight of the man in the maelstrom he has created. That is industry in the minds of many today—the Frankenstein monster, no heart, no sympathy, relentless, cruel, uncompromising, and unconquerable.

But the picture is never enduring. Today we are beginning to see another. Even industry, the monster, has its ills. A lethargy seizes it. The specialists make their diagnosis. Some say overproduction or underconsumption, and others that the trouble is improper distribution. Great masses of humanity that have been swallowed are disgorged, and we begin again to see the individual, but this time in

15

a less happy light, as a man out of work. Industry as a word conjures up a curiously changed picture.

The whole problem of unemployment is being studied as never before, and no one will deny that it merits the attention it is getting. The range of perplexing questions that it raises is almost limitless. He is indeed hardy who attempts even to enumerate them. What constitutes unemployment? Who is unemployed? How many are there out of work? Where are they? What can they do? How serious is their predicament? What can be done about it? These and a thousand other questions are asked and not yet satisfactorily answered. But no question is asked oftener now than "What of the older worker?" No question so stirs the imagination, none so sure to touch the heart as this.

The very fact that this part of the problem is close to the hearts of all of us has its effect on the statement of the case. The publicity hunter, the demagogue, and the professional politician are quick to seize on such material for their own selfish ends. Overstatement gross exaggeration, and misrepresentation, all coupled with ignorance of facts, may do more harm than good. There may be some value in the theatrical emphasis if it serves to call attention where attention is needed. It is undoubtedly of service if it brings succor that might not otherwise have been assured. But no overplay that brings as a consequence only ridicule and distrust should be encouraged. No such misrepresentation should be countenanced.

In an effort to arrive at some of the truths in the matter of the aged worker a study has for some time been going forward under the auspices of the Society of Industrial Engineers. It has been my privilege to take part in that work, and it is a pleasure to present some of the results of the survey.

This is not a new interest on the part of industrial engineers. They have placed great emphasis on increased production, and it may be that they are best known for that work. They have, however, secured that benefit for the manager while at the same time they have improved conditions for the workers. Better housekeeping, modern sanitary facilities, safety, improved lighting, and proper ventilation are always as much a part of their propaganda as is the use of the stop watch. The elimination of unnecessary fatigue and the discovery of the one best way to do work are of as much benefit to the laborer as to the manager. Thus it was from an impartial but intensely interested point of view that the welfare of the older worker was observed.

It was about six years ago that the Detroit chapter undertook a study of the methods of compensating employees for length of service. The question submitted to about one hundred firms was: "What is the best method of compensating employees for length of service, especially when they are on piece rates and are engaged in work at which their speed and consequent earning-power decreases with age?" The replies were classified into five groups, and these were described in a report printed in the *Society of Industrial Engineers' Bulletin* for March, 1924.

From time to time studies and contributions in this direction have been made by individual members and by others, at the request of the organization, and finally it was felt that a more intensive examination was warranted. As a result a questionnaire was prepared and sent out to five hundred representative industries throughout the country.

The questions submitted were basic in character and were gauged to determine the attitude of representatives of industry toward this problem, rather than to afford through the compiled answers a simple solution to a difficult situation.

Other investigations have been made, other questionnaires have been sent out, and much has been written before this, but all with a different purpose in view.

It was discovered that managers in industry are keenly interested in the problem of caring for their aged employees. Those who are selfishly interested in the problem and use its heart-interest qualities only to build up their own welfare have often attacked industry as an ingrate, who cares nothing for the man who has given his best days to her upbuilding.

The results of the survey conducted by the Society of Industrial Engineers bring forcibly to the attention the fact that there is no lack of real interest on the part of management. There is something more. Where the usual popular broadsides are loaded with suggestions for corrections, these suggestions bear the mark of the opportunist or the propagandist. The suggestions of the industrial managers show an effort at constructive thinking.

The questionnaire referred to was gauged to determine, if possible, the amount of intelligent interest that these industrial leaders took in this pressing problem. The fact that over 24 per cent of those addressed took the trouble to reply is evidence of that interest. The questions sent out required simple "yes" and "no" answers for the most part, or they might even be handled by check-marking. The interest of most of those replying did not permit such simple action. Many wrote extensively in the margins or on the backs of the sheets, and not a few contributed long and carefully written letters as evidence that they are aware of the problem and want to do something which will help in its solution.

The older employee has a friend in the industrial manager, but that does not mean that the modern mechanized processes may not overpower him in spite of that fact.

The industrial manager is concerned over this problem, but he must also keep going in the face of competition and cannot refuse to keep step with modern progress. If his employee, because of his age, finds the new tempo too fast it does not follow that that tempo must be changed, nor does it follow that nothing is to be done about it.

Nearly all the answers to the questionnaire agreed that it was inevitable in any industry that men did outlive their usefulness by simply growing old and accumulating only the ordinary quota of weaknesses of old age, but the general expression seemed to be that something might be done to shift the older employees to other departments, or to other lines of work; and one expressed the thought of many when he said, "In any vocation where a man's work requires physical vigor, the ordinary weaknesses of old age, which act as a drag, reduce his usefulness as time goes on. The only time when old age does not necessarily have this effect is when the value of a man increases with his years of experience and where the mellowing influence of time gives more and more value to his judgment."

Only a few of the industries have definite and arbitrary ages set as the maximum limit for either hiring or firing. Far the greater number are represented by the quotation from one reply: "Age is not a question of years but of condition. There are old young men and young old men. I can conceive of only a few cases, practically none, where an employee would be laid off simply because of having attained a certain age." And another: "If a man is physically and mentally able, why discharge him? To drop a man for age only is unjust. Efficiency only should be involved, regardless of age."

In answer to the question, "Do you believe that this limiting age in industry presents a general problem which should be solved?" over 80 per cent replied in the affirmative. One statement was: "In my judgment, there is no question but that group insurance, the premiums for which are figured on the average age, liability legislation, and other industrial conditions most definitely set limiting ages and that this does present a general problem which must be met."

These men representing industry were not so clear nor so united in their answers to an inquiry as to who should furnish the solution for such a problem. For the most part, responsibility was placed on the individual and not upon industry. Some felt that the state should assist, and a few included the insurance companies and the labor organizations among those groups which should co-operate in the solution of the difficulty. Many felt that the problem was for the individual, but that his ability to work his own way out would postpone the correction too long. "In my judgment," said one of the contributed replies, "it would be basically more sound for the solution to be left to the individual but this would involve the practice of some of my pet theories which do not work out. It would presume thrift, saving, intelligent investment, and a wage that would contain a fractional content for accumulated saving. In this age of instalment buying and living up one's income to the full, this is a long way from practicable."

The fact that these keen thinking men realize the possibilities of the deferred action was brought out in these answers: "The one point that should be made clear is that everything has to be paid for and that things cannot be consumed until produced, and this wave of old age pensions may sweep us off our feet if the general public is not made to realize this fact from the start." "Certain it is that under present conditions, if the bulk of our industries fail to handle properly their own business and 'pass the buck' of unemployment and old age liability on to others, they cannot complain."

Any attempt to discover what some of the causes might be which were forcing down this limiting age disclosed only that there was a divided opinion. It has been suggested that such factors as group insurance, liability legislation, and the installation of pension systems might have a tendency to restrict the use of older men in our factories. Apparently the industrial leaders are not fully convinced of this. Nearly 20 per cent were positive that these factors had no influence, and only about half of the replies indicated that those things might have an effect. "The pace in modern shops," "demand for increase of production," "higher efficiency demanded of workers on account of competition" are expressions that indicate that there might be other underlying causes affecting the situation, even though they were not the controlling elements. If the old man is not to be retained on the pay-roll, what about hiring a man who is middle-aged? There were some of the replies which indicated that managers would not hire men beyond a certain age. In this group the frank statement, "We do not hire old men," was no more easily understood than the reply, "We have no company policy on this matter at this time." It is quite evidently not necessary to establish a definite policy as to age limit, either in hiring or firing to get the same results as though such an age limit policy were established. Those indicating that they did have a definite age limit in force were about one out of every five, and the average for the limiting ages given for skilled mechanics was forty-six years, for semiskilled forty-seven years, and for the non-skilled fifty-one.

The distrust of political control and the dislike for increasing paternalism were indicated in the replies to the question as to "whether or not a scientific pension system, under state control" met with their favor. A number of suggestions were made as to what might be tried as a remedy: "Industry should take the initiative"; "industry unhampered solves this problem." These are typical of the answers which, while not conclusive as to the solution, were, in general, agreed that it was a problem and that they were willing to face it and discover, if possible, the answer.

It is quite obvious that all this study on the attitude of the industrial manager is but one part of the problem. We have started there because it seemed to be the obvious place to start. The next step may be a continuation in the same direction, and at the same time an effort may be made to branch out in other directions. The first question asked in the questionnaire submitted was one that gives rise to still another, "In the industry you represent, is it possible for men to outlive their usefulness by simply growing old and accumulating only the ordinary quota of weaknesses of old age?" This question leads to the next one, "What are the things that we would count as constituting the normal quota of weaknesses of old age?" If we agree that it is not the arbitrary age but the physical failure of the man himself that limits employment, what will determine these physical failures? Some of them we can recognize. For instance, rheumatism is obviously one of them, failing strength and lack of endurance; poor eyesight and hearing are all weaknesses in this category. Each of these weaknesses may disqualify a man for certain kinds of work and not disqualify him for others. Obviously there is presented a field for study.

What of the needs of the old man, and to what extent do these needs affect the situation? Must we wait until the needs are so great that it is simply a matter of standing between the superannuated and dire necessity? Shall we rule him out from our sympathies, if he has a family that can possibly go out into the world and earn for him a living, when under ordinary circumstances this family would be classed as dependents looking to him for their welfare? If these are children, at what age should we say they become an asset rather than a liability? At what age does the world expect them to stand ready to support the old man when he is thrown out of work? Shall the twelve-year-old leave school and sell newspapers, or shall we say that that child is still a dependent and counts simply as one more reason why the old man should be cared for?

If a man of forty-five or fifty has accumulated some savings and made possible some kind of investments, large or small, will this bar him from securing our help? If he carries insurance and on this insurance it is possible to borrow money, will we refuse to consider his plea? If he belongs to a fraternal order, shall we expect his brothers to care for him? If he has been used to a scale of living that permits him to have a radio and a Ford car, do we expect him to be reduced to the necessity of dispensing with not only these but even less important luxuries before we come to his rescue? A study of this problem cannot very well leave out the reactions of the old man himself. Will his pride permit him willingly to accept less money as he advances in years? Is he willing to change his kind of work and move to new locations, if necessary, in order to find employment? Is he anxious to work, or, if some relief is in sight, is he more apt to loaf? These things and others will determine the barriers and restrictions that will need to be put up around any form of relief that may be provided. Now as to that form of relief, should it be a pension and if a pension, should it be provided by the industry, by the state, or by some third but related group? Will it be participating or non-participating—will the whole problem be taken care of by stabilized plans—will a central employment agency answer the purpose? Can corrective factors be applied to group insurance? Can some remedy parallel to the Federal Reserve System be furnished industry to make sure that they can carry on? The type of the remedy to be applied may again be affected by the character of the agency which brings about this correction. If the correction is secured by mass action of employees through force, its character would be difficult to predict. If these same masses worked through political channels, some idea of the character of the remedy might be hazarded, but as to its value that again would be in question.

If organizations and intermediate groups handle the appeal, presumably all the questions will be given some kind of fairness in their treatment, and at the other end of the scale we have remedies which might be brought about through the action of the employers themselves. These, of course, will be the most conservative of any. Some of the bypaths will present very interesting avenues of study. For instance, what is the effect on other workers of retaining, or of not retaining, the older man? This effect can be studied through accident records, pace-making possibilities, the morale, the value of the matured counsel, and many other ways. The important thing and the plea which must be answered promptly is the cry for immediate action. Promptness with relief is just as important as its adequacy and character. If proper balancing of all these is important, surely it can be had without sacrificing the important element of timeliness.

LABOR'S POINT OF VIEW

JOHN H. WALKER

President, Illinois Federation of Labor

My experience with the industrial engineers has led me to believe that they are just as human as men in any other sphere of life. But we are all more or less influenced by our environment. As a general policy, I think, it is the best thing, even for the individual workman concerned, to strive to a greater efficiency at his job and to leave the care of the individual for general consideration.

Doing most of one's work in the office over blueprints may not always give one the sort of contacts that will enable one to see the human side of the picture; just as we who are dealing practically all the time with human beings do not always see the point of value of work that is done out in the office over blueprints. Naturally, one puts more value on the work that one is doing than on the work of the other fellow. I hope, however, that sooner or later the engineers will learn to consider the question from both sides. If they do they will accomplish a great deal. I only wish that they had started earlier, before the problem of conflicts of business and human interests had gone as far as it has.

I think it was President Roosevelt who said that you can only build the structural and spiritual values on a basis of a sound foundation of material welfare of all the people. You can't begin to get the finest out of civilization with people whose needs of life are not sufficiently met; and if only those needs are properly satisfied we might be able to get the finest quality in men.

I am rather under the impression that if you could go among the three or four millions of people who are idle in the country, men of all ages and all walks of life, the 350,000 who are idle not only in this city but in all cities, in an effort to listen to them without their knowing what we were doing, we would not hear them discussing the higher, finer things of life. They are talking, of course, of things, of food, debts, and jobs. Judge Bartelme told me some time ago that there are thousands of people without food in our city every day.

It must take a mighty strong character to keep one's mind on the finer things of life under the circumstances.

There are, of course, two kinds of unemployment, those who are unemployed because of the defect in the economic system; the other kind of unemployed are those with some personal difficulty, whether inherited or developed, within their environment. Perhaps if we were to take care entirely of those of the first group whose unemployment is due to the ineffective economic system, that might be the most important step that we could take in the right direction for giving the next generation a better heritage and better environment.

However, I recognize that we have got together here today mainly for the purpose of considering the problems of old age rather than unemployment, but may I point out in this connection that, if a man or woman who is entirely dependent upon work for his or her livelihood cannot obtain employment between the ages of forty to forty-five (which is rapidly becoming the wage-earning limit) and that age at which he may qualify for a pension, it will mean that all these men and women when they reach the pension age will become dependents. They cannot have much saved up for old age if they cannot get work after the age of forty or forty-five.

I confess, I am somewhat doubtful that we shall be able to get a pension law enacted in Illinois until there has been a complete readjustment of a state system of taxation. Our present tax law is antiquated and unfair. Under this system the farms and modest homes which present some 20 per cent of value of property in the states, pay 85 per cent; it is true that under the Constitution all property must be assessed at the same rate according to its value, but a great many stocks and bonds are not bringing any returns. To tax them in accordance with the law would amount to confiscation, so once a year almost all of us commit perjury before the tax assessor, and he knows that we are committing perjury; we defraud the states and he knows it. Not only do we not pay all that the law requires but we do not even pay all we could afford to pay as we might do if we had a reasonable system of taxation. That problem has been discussed in the legislature upon the floors of both houses repeatedly. I have heard a governor of one of the states say that a man would be foolish not to resort to perjury under such a system. Until we get a new tax law which will require people to pay their taxes on the basis of their ability to pay, it will be extremely difficult to get a satisfactory old age pension law in the state of Illinois.

Old age pension laws are in operation in every civilized country in the world, perhaps India and China are about the only two important countries, except the United States, without some old age pension. Every industrial province in Canada now has an old age pension law in operation; and even in the large agricultural provinces the prospects are good, and old age pension legislation will be enacted shortly. In Germany a system of old age pension has been in existence over forty years.

What is the situation in this country? There may be a few counties in the United States where the cost of maintaining old folks in almshouses is not greater than would be the cost of pensions; but I think that nowhere the cost of almshouses is less than the cost of a pension, and in most of county almshouses the average cost is perhaps double of what the cost of such pensions has been advocated to be. I heard Mr. Benjamin Bell state that the average cost of maintaining the poor in the Rock Island Alms House was over $50.00 a month. And he further stated that there wasn't an inmate in that almshouse, except those who are sick, who wouldn't much rather take a half-amount and live among his own people.

Mr. Bell told me that he visited Montana, where the pension law was put into operation last summer, and the governor of that state, who had opposed the old age pension law only a short while ago, admitted that he was very pleasantly surprised at the way the law was operating and that no one in Montana is opposed to the old age pension act and that it is costing the state and counties less than the other arrangements did.

Such information as I was able to gather seems to indicate that perhaps 40 per cent of those receiving pensions are mothers, women who spent their lifetime rearing children and who never had any desire in the family fortune other than spending as much as they were allowed to take care of children as best they could. When they get too old to work and have remained widows they have to go to the poorhouse.

I am not speaking out of pure imagination. I do not want to paint highly emotional pictures. The publishers of the large newspapers in your city are not running wild with human emotion and sympathy for unfortunates. My guess would be that they are inclined to lean in the other direction, yet you hardly can pick up a newspaper in Chicago without reading some story of old people who are unemployed, who have starved or frozen to death, or who have committed homicide or suicide; and what is true of Chicago is true of practically every city in the country.

There is one question that puzzles me more than anything else, and if I am wrong I would like the engineers and experts to tell me so. The experts in such different positions as Mr. Ethelbert Stewart, Secretary Davis, or Henry Ford, or such radicals as Thomas Edison or Irving Fisher, all seem to agree that as a result of the institution of machinery and other mechanical improvements our production capacity has increased so that today we could establish a six-hour day and a five-day week and produce a good deal more than we can consume on the basis of our present standard of living. Secretary Davis of the United States Department of Labor made the statement, which is supported by many well-informed men, that the era of invention and discovery and the improvement in production has only begun, that every day sees many improvements in the same direction, and that as time goes on power-driven machinery will more and more displace hard physical labor formerly performed by human hands. Secretary Davis says that, when machinery displaces human labor, it is good business not to discharge the workers because discharging them would force millions of people out of labor and they would have no buying capacity. It is better business, he claims, to keep them employed until they find some other work. What happens now is that, when the thousands upon thousands of aged men and women do not have their needs supplied from industries which could supply those needs but remain idle, decent folks contribute out of what little they have to keep others alive. They reduce their own purchasing capacity as a result, and there is more idleness in industry, the owner loses the business and profits, the merchants lose their business and profits, the worker loses the work and wages, and the professional man cannot render his services to the wage-earner because he is unable to pay for it. If all the effective needs were supplied, what would happen is that the industries would be stimulated to greater productivity, the employer would get his profits, and the merchant would get his business, and the wage-earner would get his work and his wages, the professional man would get his work, and everybody would profit, because misery could be avoided or reduced. If that is true—and I have discussed the question with many workers and with some industrial managers and no one seems to disagree—then it is not only a reflection upon our humanity but upon our intellect not to supply these needs. No one profits when the needy people, whether they be aged or unemployed, remain in want; but everybody would profit as their needs were supplied. Those who have delved deepest into the problems and understand it best of all have agreed that this age of increased efficiency and power-driven machinery is offering us an opportunity to bring about a civilization on a higher plane than has ever been dreamt of by human beings. On the other hand, if we fail to take advantage of these opportunities it may bring the ugliest picture to us that has ever been written in human history.

It is hard enough to deal with criminals, but with some force they can be dealt with fairly successfully or at least they can be restrained; but take three or four millions of decent men who are able to work, willing to work, anxious to work, but can't find work, and if you allow them and their families to suffer, if you keep a large number of men of that kind idle long enough, mark my word, there isn't any criminal that will create so much destruction as they will; for decent fine men who are willing to work, who want to do the thing that is right and can't get the opportunity, men who suffer and who see their families suffer, men who on the whole are more intellectual than the criminal, when they make up their minds to go wrong, they will not consider the consequences. That is the greatest menace, the greatest threat to civilization. And the most pitiable thing of it all is that it is altogether unnecessary.

I have no doubt that if we could have our children all go to high school after they are graduated from common school rather than to work at the age of fourteen it would be the best influence we could have. If we were to make the high-school certificate take the place of grade-school certificates, they might then find enough work for adults.

After all, it is the owners of the industries in your city who determine what the working hours and working wages should be. They are those who have the power and responsibility for the difficulties inherent in the economic system. If evil comes out of this situation, on their shoulders will be the greatest amount of responsibility. Efficiency should reduce to a minimum those who ought to work and want to work and can't find work. But we must furnish them employment when they are young and able to work. We must furnish them adequate wages so that they can live as they should and can be provided for in their old age. Unemployment and low wages are responsible for the number of old age dependents. Unemployment and low wages are contributing factors because they not only make pension services impossible but also, because insufficient wages prevent the working masses from buying the goods they need, reduce the market for all industry and thus cause unemployment. All these complicating factors must be taken into consideration if an intelligent understanding is to be worked out. If I understand the temperament of men and women who are in responsible positions and hold the real power in our social life (and I think I do after thirty years of association with them), they want to avoid doing or saying anything that will bring trouble to our country. They want to use their influence to meet problems peacefully, intelligently, and decently. They want to achieve an adjustment of the problem arising out of productivity of high-power machinery so as to enable them to get full benefit without causing any injury to anybody. If these men and women will only try to get at the facts, to consider them with open minds, to deal with them intelligently, if they will put themselves in the position of those other men and women who suffer from unemployment and old age, if only both sides will try to get together, then I hope in a very short time this will eliminate the possibility of riots and parades of the unemployed; but something definite must be done in that direction. Otherwise we are still running very serious risks.

INSTITUTIONAL CARE OF THE AGED

C. B. COSGROVE

Superintendent, Home for Dependents, Welfare Island, New York City

The subject assigned to me, the "Care of the Aged in Institutions," is one that has been talked about during the past ten years from almost every angle. There is one group who cry "Away with the institutions. An old man or woman must not be shamed by being put in a county or city home. They must be provided with means to maintain themselves in their own homes and in the style to which they have been accustomed." There is another group who declare that the institution is the only possible way in which an old man or woman can be properly cared for.

I have been thirty-three years with my department, and at least twenty of these have been devoted to the care of the aged; at first without the walls of the institution, and for the last eleven years, as the head of what is the largest institution of its kind in the world. Including the Chronic Hospital and Cancer Hospital, there is under the care of the institution today a total of more than thirty-seven hundred dependents; men and women who, in one way or another, have contributed their bit toward the support and development of the city of New York. It is possibly true that some of these men and women never did earn a dollar in all their lives, but they did exist and someone was provided with work in order to provide for them. The habitual drunkard helped support the bartender and the saloon keeper; and if *they* did nothing else toward the benefit of the community, they at least paid taxes. Even the prohibition drunkard helps the bootlegger to acquire the luxuries incidental to a large fortune, to enable him to buy expensive cars, to live expensively, and to this extent to swell the income of the community and consequently contribute to its development. It seems to me impossible for any human being to live for any length of time without in some way aiding the general welfare. It follows then, that no matter what the former mode of living of an old man or old woman may have been, they are, when they reach the age of dependency, legitimately wards of the community at large; and it is, without a question, the duty of the community to make such provision as will make them most comfortable and happy during the remainder of their lives irrespective of their social status previous to dependency.

From time immemorial, this provision has been made by providing shelter in monasteries, convents, workhouses, almshouses, jails, and later by church charities, parish visitors, private charitable societies and by the community itself in city homes, county homes, and similarly euphoniously named institutions. It is an unfortunate phase of the situation that even in the building of modern homes for the aged, we are unable entirely to divest ourselves of the age-old tradition that an old man requires nothing more than shelter, food, clothing of a sort, and the privilege of dying peacefully as far away from the public gaze as it is possible to get him. He has been looked upon as a piece of worn-out machinery that has passed from the workshop of life to the most available junk-pile where he is allowed slowly to rust out his existence with such occasional treatments as may be necessary to make the process as painless as possible.

The department of hospitals in New York, under the active leadership of its present commissioner, the Hon. J. G. William Greeff, M.D., is determined to break away from this tradition and to provide a home that will possess the comfort and privacy the name implies and at the same time provide the conveniences and facilities for proper care that are necessary in an institution. Even the most modern institutions that I know of lose sight of the fact that there are times when every man and woman wants to be alone. The most gregarious of us tire of the crowd, and, if we are alone at no other time, we at least attain a reasonable measure of release from our fellows while asleep. To the inmate of the so-called "homes" even this is denied. In our own institution from twenty to one hundred and forty persons are sleeping in one room. Between five hundred and six hundred of them eat in one dining-room. From twelve to thirty of them bathe at one time. At no time during the day or night can they find themselves by themselves, and the lack of privacy seems to me to be one of the things that most leads to discontent.

Instead of these large congregate homes, we are considering a development at the Staten Island branch of the institution which will cost approximately five millions of dollars. The first four units of the new institution have been planned. The largest number of men or women grouped together is four, and the beds are so arranged that it will be possible to provide for each individual, visual privacy at least. This is a long step in the right direction; but, in addition to this, the further development will be along the lines of the family cottage plan in which comparatively small groups, possibly as small as ten or fifteen individuals, carefully selected for their congeniality, will be housed with a house government of their own similar to that maintained at any well-organized club. While we are endeavoring to give to our prospective dependents the best and the most comfortable quarters that we can, we must bear in mind that the institution is supported by the taxpayers, is largely an unproductive investment, must be capable of economical administration, and for this reason we are planning a common dining-room and, of course, common kitchen. The dining-room, however, is so designed that it will be possible to group the residents of each building by themselves and in this way escape the unpleasant features due to the various standards of table manners unavoidable in the large open dining-rooms of an institution. Such an arrangement would, of course, lend itself most readily to the correction of another disagreeable feature of congregate institution life. I refer to the lack of individual clothing. It is practically impossible, under existing conditions, for a man or woman to get the same suit or dress or underwear the second time; and when one considers the overcrowded quarters, insufficient help, the impatience of the old man or woman, it is remarkable that the clothing furnished is approximately the right size. At present it would be hopeless to attempt to provide individual clothing. Under the proposed plan with its grouping of small "families" there will be no difficulty in so doing, and possibly one of the most irritating of the existing features will be eliminated. The inmates of a home such as the Home for Dependents of New York represent a cross-section of the community life. The population is made up of professional men and women, of cashiers, clerks, sales people, skilled tradesmen, unskilled workers of both sexes, and unemployable men and women. Lawyers, doctors, teachers, politicians, every walk of life is represented at one time or another, and in planning an institution for their care, due consideration should be given to this important fact.

It seems to me that the time has come when we must get away from the practice of spending as little money as possible and adopt a new policy of spending as much money as possible, wisely. If we do so, the question of institutional care of the aged will settle itself.

At the beginning of these remarks I referred to a group of people who desire to see the institution entirely abolished. My experience has taught me that this is impossible. A very small proportion, probably not more than 10 per cent of all those who reach the age of dependency, can be properly cared for outside of an institution, whether that institution be a home for the aged or a hospital for the treatment of chronic diseases. Even in the case of the man or woman whose family relationships are of an amiable character, it is difficult for a son-in-law or daughter-in-law, or grandchild to accept the presence and the whims of the senescent. It is equally difficult for the aged person to realize that the home in which he finds himself is no longer his. That, instead of being the head of the house, he has become a member of the family and that the son or daughter whom he has been accustomed to dominate has now become the arbiter of the household destinies. He is constantly in a resentful frame of mind. He feels slighted and does not hesitate to voice his irritation or his opinion at the most inopportune moments. An inferiority complex, in other words, forces him into an attitude of constant self-assertion with a resultant family row. The old man is uncomfortable, the younger people unhappy, and the situation at its best is always at the breaking-point.

This would be true even if the old man was only partially dependent since there would be a continual effort on his part to control the expenditures of whatever income he might have. It is, of course, readily understandable that, with an income insufficient to provide complete maintenance, the only practical thing under such circumstances would be a pooling of all the resources of the family group and its wise expenditure through one source. In our American life this seems to be the wife whom I have learned to recognize as the head of the household; the husband is, of course, the neck, inasmuch as he supports the head. Such control of what he considers his own money is always resented by the old man and leads to continual friction. There is a feeling through the house generally that the old man or woman should be content to sit by themselves and not interfere with the general household life. Their ideas are out of date, they dislike noise, they do not approve of the friends of the younger members of the family, they hate to be kept awake after their bed hour by talking and laughing. They have been known to appear unexpectedly in their nightclothes at parties, much to the detriment of the pleasure of the evening. They do not, to put it briefly, fit in. They should be and can be best cared for with others having their own or similar infirmities and views on life.

I know, of course, that there are men and women of advanced years whose life is a perfect picture of peace and happiness; whose presence in the family circle is welcome at any and all times; whose existence is a perfect example of the blessing of adaptability; whose death would be a real loss not only to their own immediate family but to that family's circle of acquaintances. We all know such men and women, particularly women. But such men and such women do not become dependents in any sense. They have, without any effort on their own part, because of their character and disposition, made an investment and one far surer in its returns and far more effective for their comfort and happiness than any mere monetary investment could possibly be. They cannot, and must not, be put forward as examples of the general condition. It is a regrettable fact that in the great majority of instances, these happy conditions do not exist, and any provision that is made for old age security must take these facts into consideration.

It would be of interest, perhaps, to know what New York City does for its aged guests. A complete physical examination is made of each new arrival on the day following admission. The result of this examination determines the individual's status. If he requires hospital care he is assigned to the hospital division. If not, it fixes his ability to work, if any, and indicates the amount of work he can be safely given to do.

The hospital division is fully equipped. The Cancer Hospital, for which the city purchased $140,000 worth of radium, is supplied with everything necessary for the treatment and comfort of its patients. Nursing supervision is provided in the Home proper. A dispensary is maintained for such as do not require hospital care. Morning and afternoon "sick lines" are seen by a doctor.

The institution costs the city of New York approximately $1,250,000 a year yet the per capita per diem cost is only $1.09. Every charge, except interest on original investment, is included in this.

We maintain, for the care of personal effects, a well-organized property system including a non-interest-paying banking system with 613 active accounts and an average balance of $14,000. Depositors are privileged to deposit and draw as often as they wish. The officers of the Home conduct a community store at which candy, tobacco, notions, etc., may be purchased. The profits are applied to the Welfare Fund.

A social service division, established two and a half years ago, is proving most useful and successful. Already some two hundred persons have been placed in what seems to be permanent employment. At least they have not applied for readmission—they are no longer dependent. This division is also of service in straightening difficulties with insurance policies; re-establishes family contacts; supplies, in short, a most useful connection with the outside world.

We have practically no rules, no disciplinary measures except discharge from the Home—a rarely resorted to punishment. Guests have direct access to the superintendent. He has acquired a bottomless ear, and it is surprising how speedily troubles disappear when poured into it.

Twice a week we have "Talkies"—pictures shown from the best current releases. The program contains a "feature," a comedy, and a news reel.

During the winter season, the National Vaudeville Association furnishes entertainments, frequently bringing over the entire program from one of the city theaters.

A number of fraternal societies give us an opportunity to see and hear their minstrel shows, plays, etc. A master radio set, equipped with thirty-eight loud speakers and two hundred and fifty pairs of ear-phones, brings in the best programs.

INSTITUTIONAL CARE OF THE AGED
IN THE UNITED STATES

FLORENCE E. PARKER

U.S. Bureau of Labor Statistics, Washington, D.C.

Last year a special study of homes for the aged was made by the United States Bureau of Labor Statistics. After inquiry of all the sources that were potential avenues of information, we built up a list of 1,270 homes. No doubt a town-to-town canvass would reveal the existence of many more, but this we were unable to undertake. Reports were received from 1,037 homes housing some 69,000 persons. In addition, visits were made to some 150 homes, in order to see the actual conditions under which the old people were living. No attempt was made at selection of the homes visited. The area of Maryland, Connecticut, and the eastern half of Pennsylvania was selected as affording a representative industrial and agricultural section, and within that area every home was visited. Later, a supplementary study was made on the special point of what the homes were doing to keep their old people occupied.

About 100 of the homes were supported by fraternal organizations, more than 400 by churches or religious groups, 33 by groups of various nationalities (French, English, Scotch, Swiss, Czechoslovak, etc.), 38 by various organizations such as the Ladies of the G. A. R., Women's Christian Association, Y. W. C. A., associations for the deaf, etc., 5 by trade-unions, 55 by the Federal or state governments, and 360 by groups of philanthropic citizens.

In order to enter a home the applicant must comply with certain requirements as to physical condition, age, property, residence, membership in a specified organization, etc. Certain homes accept only men, others only women, but nearly 60 per cent of the total take both sexes. Nearly half of the homes make no financial demands upon the applicant, but others require a regular weekly or monthly board or an entrance fee (most commonly of $500, but in some instances running up to several thousand dollars). In many cases, also, the residents are expected to lend their services at small duties around the home.

The entrance requirements usually limit the field from which the residents are accepted—in some cases so greatly as to curtail considerably the usefulness of the home as a factor in the problem of the care of the aged. I have in mind a home of considerable size, beautifully situated and tastefully furnished, which accepts only Presbyterian ministers who do not use tobacco in any form. The home has had no occupants for several years, although it is situated in a territory in which nearly all the other homes have a long waiting list.

The visits to the homes were very interesting, covering all types and all degrees of comfort or lack of it. At one extreme is a home, lavishly endowed under the will of a rich man, which stands in large landscaped grounds, in a beautiful residential suburb. The living rooms are the last word in comfort and even luxury. Each inmate has his own bedroom which is furnished with soft, thick carpet, easy chairs, several floor and wall lights, individual telephone, four-poster bed, chiffonier, bookcases, fireplace, and a clothes closet equipped with both shelves and drawers. Each room has a toilet in connection. The home will accommodate 80, but the entrance requirements are so strict and the character and other qualifications so high that so far only 21 applicants have been admitted and there is one section of the house which the management has not yet furnished.

At the other end of the scale are the homes which usually have no requirements except age and destitution. These furnish only cleanliness and the barest necessaries of existence—the plainest food, and sleeping accommodations in large dormitories holding as many as 30 or 35 beds. In such homes there is practically no privacy, practically nothing in the way of comforts, and in some institutions of this type a splint rocker is regarded as a luxury. For the class of persons admitted, the assurance of food and shelter even of the poorest sort must be a blessing, but one visiting these homes cannot help but pity the old, tired bodies that must rest themselves in hard straight chairs, especially where the dormitories are locked during the day, as was found to be the case in several instances.

The average home, however, stands midway between these

extremes. The living rooms are generally comfortably furnished with well-worn furniture, the food is good and plentiful, though plain, and generally individual bedrooms are assigned. There seems to be a very general desire on the part of the matrons of these institutions to make the place a real home.

I should like to say a word in tribute to the work the matrons are doing. Anyone, even without experience in this line, can imagine the task of harmonizing the tastes and wants of anywhere from 10 to 200 old people, each with settled habits and opinions. Some old persons are very sweet and easy to get on with, but some are anything else but, and the matron of an old people's home gets both kinds. True, the homes always reserve the right to expel any individual who is too difficult, but the matron will generally put up with a great deal rather than go to the length of requesting the removal of an inmate.

These matrons generally take an active and intelligent interest in their jobs. I found any number who were well-informed in regard to all the homes in their locality and one or two who had spent some of their vacations visiting other homes to get "pointers" as to how their own institutions might be improved. Their interest is also indicated by the fact that of the 1,270 homes to which questionnaires were sent, returns were received from nearly 82 per cent—which is a very high rate of return in questionnaire studies. One fault is that many feel pride in the fact of the inmates' having "nothing to do but enjoy themselves," and fail to see that that very condition is in itself bad for the old people who are still active. It was this fact, coupled with the obvious effects of lack of mental occupation, found in some of the homes visited, that led to the third part of our study— that of the problem of idleness in old people's homes.

As I have said, we found that the resident population of the 1,037 homes was nearly 69,000 persons. On the basis of the average population of the homes reporting, we estimate that homes for the aged in the United States have facilities for 80,000 persons. That they cannot begin to meet the need existing is shown by the fact that practically 90 per cent of the homes that were visited had long waiting lists—so long that it may take years for an applicant to obtain admittance to the home. It is possible that this condition does not obtain in other sections of the country which were not visited, but I doubt it.

The average per capita cost of operation of the homes reporting was $437.57. This average is undoubtedly affected by the fact that it was generally the homes which were the better managed and the more prosperous which furnished expense data. On the other hand, this figure does not include interest on money invested in building and lands, nor, in some cases, the total cost of medical care, for much of the medical attention is given free by the local physicians. However, it may be said that the above average represents a fairly liberal amount which will provide all necessaries and plain comfort.

In this connection it might be observed that in a study of cost of operation of almshouses made by the Bureau of Labor Statistics several years ago, it was found that the average annual per capita cost was $334.64. This figure, also, did not include interest on the money invested in land, buildings, and equipment. If interest be included, the total average cost to the public per inmate was $439.76. This is interesting in view of the relative comforts provided by the two classes of institutions—homes and almshouses—to say nothing of the loss of self-respect involved in being committed to an almshouse.

THE CARE OF THE AGED SICK

ERNST P. BOAS, M.D.

New York City

The problem of old age is largely a problem of sickness. Although death-rates have fallen dramatically in recent decades and although the average expectancy of life at birth is greatly increased, the mortality in the later years of life has shown no improvement. As a matter of fact, because more persons reach old age the absolute number of those afflicted with the diseases of this period of life is on the increase. In European countries, where highly developed old age pension systems afford relief during the period of senility, there are usually more individuals receiving invalidity pensions than old age pensions. In the almshouses barely 15 per cent of the aged inmates are in sound or fair health, and in the homes for the aged fully one-third are infirmary patients. Of these about one-half are bedridden. When it is recognized that ill health is the major cause of financial dependency at all age periods, it is clear that any study of the needs of the aged must concern itself closely with the nature and significance of the diseases to which these old people are subject.

These diseases are primarily the chronic degenerative diseases. They begin to take their toll in the sixth decade and become increasingly frequent in the succeeding years. True aging is the result of the gradual wearing out and enfeeblement of the organs and tissues of the body, and rarely becomes manifest before the age of seventy. Most of the disabilities of the sixth and seventh decades of life are caused by chronic disease, by a deterioration of some vital organ or organ system, long before the rest of the body is anatomically or physiologically senescent. Yet by common usage they are identified with the process of physiological aging. As a consequence individuals between their fiftieth and seventieth years who are disabled and infirm are all too often regarded as senile rather than as sick. The community contents itself with providing them with simple custodial care, which is totally inadequate, instead of with the medical attention that they need. The first step, then, to an appreciation of the significance of chronic diseases as a factor in the care of the aged involves an exact understanding of their nature and prevalence, as well as a restriction of the term "senile" to true physiological aging.

What are the diseases that contribute chiefly to the invalidity of the aged? In the order of their importance they are: organic heart disease, cerebral hemorrhage or apoplexy, Bright's disease, cancer, and diseases of the arteries. Together they are responsible for nearly 70 per cent of all deaths occurring after the age of sixty-five. In view of the fact that cerebral hemorrhage and Bright's disease in the elderly are almost always associated with, or determined by, disease of the heart and arteries, it appears that over one-half of all deaths are caused by diseases of the cardiovascular system. In these older age groups the degenerative diseases of the heart and blood vessels hold sway—hardening of the arteries, with its manifold consequences, and high blood pressure. Other diseases of importance are the non-tuberculous diseases of the lung, such as emphysema, chronic bronchitis and asthma, diabetes mellitus, chronic rheumatism, and disorders of the brain and spinal cord resulting in all types of paralysis and disability.

Acute diseases have a self-limited course; there is a rapid evolution toward recovery or death. Chronic diseases are insidious in their onset and slowly progressive; their course extends over months or years; there may be arrest of the morbid process; but there is never complete restoration to normal. For the most part they are diseases of obscure origin, although a number of the infectious diseases, in particular tuberculosis, syphilis, and the several forms of rheumatism, are responsible for much chronic disability.

Chronic diseases differ from acute diseases, not alone in their essential medical characteristics, but in their social and economic consequences as well. In most acute disease medical considerations are paramount; compared with them the social and economic difficulties are temporary and unimportant. In chronic disease the medical, social, and economic elements are inextricably interwoven and of equal significance. The direct cost of caring for the sick is a considerable item, when charges for physicians and nurses, special foodstuffs, medicines, and sickroom supplies are constantly recurring for periods of months. When the resources of legitimate medicine seem to bring no relief, these chronic invalids readily become the victims of various quacks and cultists who exploit them ruthlessly.

When the wage-earner himself is ill, the principal income is lost to the family; and, if there are no savings, complete destitution soon follows. Relatives can help in emergencies, but rarely can such assistance be extended over long periods of time. The wife or some other potential or actual wage-earner must stay at home to care for the invalid. If it is not the chief wage-earner who is ill, the situation is not so desperate, but in the course of time it exerts its inevitable drag. The provider himself may have to stay at home from time to time because of the disorganization resulting from the illness; he may have to employ a woman to help in the home; he may have to board out his children; he may be taxed in innumerable ways. With it all he is harassed by worry, his sleep may be interfered with, so that eventually he may succumb physically and spiritually to the long continued strain.

Prolonged illness places as great a strain on the varied human relationships comprised in a family as any other factor. The parents become such a burden to the younger generation that, after a while, the children welcome any means that will enable them to be rid of them. Not infrequently it is the son-in-law or the daughter-in-law who will not tolerate the presence of the invalid in the home. The patient himself may be so exacting in his demands and so self-centered that home care becomes impossible even when the relatives are considerate and willing. Among the poor with a large family forced to live in a few small rooms, the situation often becomes intolerable. Quite aside from the financial burden, the constant presence of the invalid, who may be querulous and exacting and who must often be tended at night, is a constant drain on the vitality of the members of his family. Night after night, a mother, a father, a daughter, or a son may have his sleep interrupted by the calls of the patient; the whole atmosphere of the home becomes subdued, the children lose their spontaneity, and life assumes a dull and drab color. A daughter or, more rarely, a son may be compelled to postpone marriage for years because of the burden of the sick parent.

Because of all of these factors, we see family after family disorganized, with shattered morale and resultant destitution.

These ill effects are not confined to the patient and to his family alone, but are a drain on the community resources as well. Various social agencies are called on to give relief. There is no organization doing welfare work, be it family welfare, social service, or district nursing group, no hospital, dispensary, or home for the aged or incurable that is not called on daily to solve problems arising from the immediate effects and by-products of chronic invalidism.

Sufferers from chronic organic disease offer much the same problem as do the tuberculous and the insane, i.e., social and economic factors interplaying with medical ones. For the latter two groups fairly adequate provisions have been made, because the mentally deranged and the tuberculous offer a greater immediate menace to the community. Hospitals for the insane and sanatoriums for the tuberculous all over the country give protracted medical and domiciliary care to these sufferers at the expense of the community. The patient receives a fighting chance, and his family is eased from an excessive burden. This same humane policy should be extended to the victim of chronic organic disease. We must recognize that the chronic sick cannot shift for themselves, that the problem by far exceeds the capacity of private relief organizations, and that it is a matter for organized public relief.

How are the needs of the chronic sick to be met, and, in particular, how shall the sick aged be cared for? The aged may be divided into the able-bodied and the sick. The able-bodied do not come in the province of this discussion; their troubles are primarily social and economic, and must eventually be met by some far-reaching scheme of old age pensions. There is a group of the aged, who, while not sick, are suffering from such physical and mental enfeeblement that they need some very simple supervision and assistance. This we may call aged care. Then there is the group that is still ambulant, though suffering from some concrete disability, who can be treated by their private physicians, if they have money to pay them, who else must be cared for in out-patient clinics. This type of care will become more significant with the provision of some pension system, as well as with the rapid improvement of the out-patient departments.

Those of the chronic sick whose disablement is farther advanced have been classed in three main groups: Class A, those requiring medical care for diagnosis and treatment; Class B, those requiring chiefly skilled nursing care; Class C, those requiring only custodial care. These different types of care may be given at home or in an institution. While members of Class A are probably always best served in an appropriate institution, individuals belonging to the other two groups may be cared for either within or without an institution. The determining factors here are only in part medical. Of course if the patients are very helpless and need a great deal of nursing, institutional care will be necessary. But for those who are not so physically dependent, the economic and social circumstances will be the deciding ones.

If conditions are at all favorable, many of these patients can well be looked after in their own homes, or they may be placed as boarders in suitable homes, provided a well-organized visiting nurse system exists to insure adequate care. At the present time many chronic patients do receive such home care supervised and assisted by visiting nurses. A recent survey by the Welfare Council in New York City showed that nearly one-third of the chronic sick discovered in the census were under the care of community nursing agencies. However, the Welfare Council's Section on Public Health Nursing itself stated that "because of the increased demand for the services of trained visiting nurses to acutely ill patients during certain seasons of the year, the chronic sick do not receive adequate care." An important measure, therefore, is a further extension of the visiting nurse system for the relief of the chronic sick. For many patients, women less highly trained than nurses, carefully supervised by graduate nurses, might provide very valuable service at less cost.

For the sicker patients, and for those who have no homes, or whose home environment is impossible for one reason or another, institutional care becomes necessary. At present many types of institutions: homes for the aged, homes for incurables, almshouses, city or county infirmaries, offer refuge to these unfortunates without meeting their needs. To understand the institutional resources demanded by the chronic sick, we must again revert to our classification. The two great groups are those needing active medical or nursing care and those needing simple domiciliary care. The first need all of the resources of a general hospital placed at their disposal for extended periods of time; they must be harbored in hospitals for chronic diseases. The second need only domiciliary care; they require nothing but a home, so constructed and managed that the physical handicaps of the patients do not result in their becoming involuntary prisoners in their rooms. Since the medical condition of these sick people is constantly changing, since one month they may need much attention, and then again for a period of time only custody, opportunities must be provided for a free transfer from one type of institution to another.

How well is this ideal institutional plan being met at present? The homes for the aged try to admit only able-bodied applicants above the age of sixty or sixty-five, and try to avoid the whole problem of chronic disease—yet with scant success. The fact remains that every institution caring for the aged, no matter how carefully it attempts to select its inmates, must deal with chronic disease as a major problem. The institutions, as a rule, retain inmates who become ill after their admission, and as a matter of fact nearly one-third of the inmates of homes for the aged are sick. Yet many of the homes have not met their obligations to the sick aged, and have not provided satisfactory medical service for them. It seems to me that there should be a fundamental reorientation in policy in institutions for the aged. The able-bodied aged should be kept in their homes through a subsidy or pension system. Only such of the aged who because of medical necessity or economic or social circumstance cannot be maintained outside of an institution should be admitted as institutional wards. The age limit should not be so inflexible, and some of the custodial chronic sick of the younger age groups, for instance those above fifty, should be admitted. With this, of course, the home would have to be prepared to give more general medical supervision and more nursing care. But it would then be serving a more vital need of the community.

The homes for incurables, too, are operating blindly. While they try to limit their admissions to the custodial class of chronic sick, they do not succeed in drawing the line so sharply. Consequently, we find many patients under their care who require active medical treatment. Yet the homes for incurables, with few exceptions, lack all medical facilities. Since it is impossible to limit the type of patient, largely because complications and reactivations of disease are very common among them, every home for incurables must have a well-organized infirmary service with doctors and nurses in attendance, or else must establish a close *liaison* with a hospital which will make possible the transfer of the sick. Ideally a home for incurables should have no separate existence, but should function as the custodial section of a hospital for chronic diseases. It is to be hoped, too, that these institutions will manifest the first glimmering of enlightenment by changing their name to one that is less forbidding and discouraging.

The almshouses share all the faults and evils of the homes for the aged and incurable without any of their virtues. They are catch-alls for a most variegated population with widely diverging needs, and are the final refuge for the majority of the aged sick. Almshouse statistics show that most of their inmates are sick; about 75 per cent of them are suffering from some chronic disease. Yet they receive almost no medical care. An analysis of the customs and practices of the almshouses, their administrative methods, and housing facilities shows them to be antiquated survivals of medieval institutions. It forcibly demonstrates the necessity and urgency of a modernization of the state's provisions for the chronically ill. It is true, in some of the larger towns and cities, the poorhouse is beginning to be equipped with facilities for the sick, and in some states the legal term for almshouse is "infirmary."

One of the difficulties delaying reform is the multiplicity of small almshouses which cannot afford to provide satisfactory service. It is tradition alone that insists that each county must have its own poorhouse. It would seem more rational for several counties to unite and, scrapping their individual almshouses, provide one adequate and central hospital for chronic diseases. Again it may be found more expedient for the state to assume this duty and to maintain at strategic geographical points a number of large and complete hospitals for chronic diseases, analogous to the state hospitals for the insane.

The hospital for chronic diseases, to which we often have made reference, is the ideal institution for those of the chronic sick who cannot be sheltered in their homes. It consists of a hospital section with all the equipment and all the medical services of a general hospital, but in which the patients are retained so long as they need medical treatment. Attached to it as an integral part is a custodial section in which are harbored the Class C cases, those of the chronic sick whose disease is arrested but who need elementary domiciliary care. Patients are transferred from one section of the hospital to the other in correspondence with their medical needs.

We have shown the overwhelming importance of the factor of illness in the care of the aged, how vitally it enters into all measures that are taken for their relief. It is illness that so often determines dependency in these people. The public at large, and the relief agencies in particular, have not given adequate recognition to this fact. A solution of the problem requires appreciation of the reciprocal relation between chronic disease and poverty, and involves both economic and medical adjustments. Once this fundamental point of view is accepted by all those who try to give assistance to the aged, it will be found that many of our present agencies can be used as starting points, and with improvement and amplification can satisfactorily serve the needs of many of the aged. Thus some form of pension system will enable many of those less severely disabled to be treated in their homes; an extension of the visiting nurse system will greatly enlarge this group, and will insure fair treatment to all the extra-institutional cases. A recognition by the homes for the aged and incurable of their proper place in the whole scheme of things will result in fewer of the able-bodied aged becoming institutional charges, and in the admission of a larger number of the really disabled custodial type of chronic sick. Finally the almshouse and city infirmary, which after all have to bear the brunt of responsibility for the care of the sick aged, will shed their medieval traditions and gradually evolve into high-class hospitals for chronic diseases. Only when the community has integrated all these resources and activities into one harmonious whole, will it be able to claim that it cares for its aged sick.

SOME MEDICAL ASPECTS OF THE CARE OF
THE AGED

MICHAEL M. DAVIS
Director for Medical Services, Julius Rosenwald Fund

Many speakers at this conference have brought out that improvement in the care of the aged is largely a problem of individualization. This applies particularly in the medical field because the care of illness is so pre-eminently an individual matter. Since a considerable proportion of aged persons must be in institutions of one kind or another, a good deal of medical care furnished the aged must be supplied under institutional conditions. It must be organized medical service; but let us give heed to the principle that we must organize with the aim of individualization and not as if we were to turn out automobiles from a moving assembly belt.

The big step in individualization from this point of view is the classification of cases according to the nature of the medical needs which they present. Everyone here recognizes what a great contribution Dr. Ernst Boas made when he established, in practice as well as theory, the simple, but fundamentally important, distinction between three types of the chronic sick: (a) those who need the resources of a hospital, (b) the slightly incapacitated who need nursing attention, but only occasional medical care, and (c) the custodial group, who can usually look after themselves physically. Many of the aged, of course, are not chronically sick, and a medical classification of the aged would include an additional group (d) who under suitable conditions, as in a home, can take a part in the social and to some extent in the economic activity of a family or community.

In the medical care of old people, we must move beyond a simple four-part classification to a more detailed individualization of the medical problem. The difficulty here is chiefly the small number of physicians who have had sufficient training or experience in the medical problems of old age or who have any real interest in these patients. For some time to come it seems hopeless to expect that, in

47

anywhere but a comparatively few large institutions in important cities, we can find physicians who will be keen on the job of looking after old people. A physician dealing with the aged ought to have the attitude of trying to see how much can be made of the old person's life. The prevalent point of view seems to be that you cannot do much for old people anyway, except palliation when their aches and pains become acute. We need, among the physicians who are responsible for the care of a group of aged persons, both a special interest and skill in the disease problems of old persons and also the point of view of what Samuel Hopkins Adams years ago called the "health master," the physician who tried to help people make the most of themselves physically.

The cost of adequate institutional care for the aged will increase substantially if we pass from a merely custodial to a hospital basis and is hardly thinkable unless the institutions are units of 250 beds and more. Otherwise, the laboratory facilities, physiotherapy and the technical personnel required for adequate attention require too large an overhead. The only solution of medical care for the chronic sick and for those aged who are chronically sick and need hospital attention is the development of chronic divisions in conjunction with general hospitals. Only in cities of half a million population and over can we expect to have adequately equipped medical institutions especially and solely for the chronic sick and aged.

The medical care of the aged at home presents a three-fold problem: facilities, supervision, and family adjustment. My own point of view is strongly in favor of emphasizing in every possible way the opportunities of home care for the aged as distinguished from institutional care. With the aged who fall into the custodial group and some of those in Dr. Boas' (b) group, home care is physically possible. For the (a) group, the chronic sick, it is impracticable or at least is bound to be inadequate.

Old age pensions would furnish an economic basis on which the home care of the aged might be largely extended; and the relative economy of this, as compared with institutional care, is an important argument for pension systems.

The adjustment of the old person in his own family or into the families of what might be called "foster homes" for the aged is essentially a problem of mental hygiene. That most fashionable branch of medicine today, psychiatry, has laid emphasis mainly upon the child, is beginning to pay systematic attention to young persons in schools and colleges; but among adults extends to few except those who are able to afford psychic luxuries at from $10 to $25 per hour. When the present generation of psychiatrists begins itself to approach senescence, perhaps the weight of years and authority will be lent to encouraging the succeeding generation in the science to devote attention to the mental hygiene of those approaching three-score and ten.

The real problem of mental hygiene of the aged, however, is largely one of family adjustment to the aged person. This adjustment is at least as much, perhaps more, to be made by the children and middle-aged people in the family rather than by the aged person himself. The program of mental hygiene for the adolescent and the young adult ought to include imaginative forecasts, under psychiatrically directed mental massages, of what old age may be like if we shape our minds so as to make it so. Sympathetic adjustment to the crotchets and foibles of the old is infinitely easier for those who appreciate that old persons are ourselves, plus a few years. People who have such appreciation will, moreover, develop fewer crotchets as they grow hoary. Young persons thus disciplined will when approaching senility have a more satisfactory background and mental attitude than the aged person of today generally possesses. The old person must neither expect too much for himself nor should too much or too little be expected of him.

I plead, then, for including in your program for the care of the aged some real attention to the mental hygiene of senescence as the basis of more extended and more satisfactory home care and of a happier family life for and with the aged, and I beg to call to your attention my belief that the preparation for wholesome attitudes when old begins with the mental hygiene of youth.

DISCUSSION

JAMES MULLENBACH

Chicago

Anyone acquainted with the population of our larger county infirmaries or institutions will realize that there are certain elements of the population that will always need institutional care. Practically all inmates of the "irresponsible" or neurological wards, patients in advanced degrees of cancer, tuberculosis, and other chronic diseases, imbecile children and the idiots are among those who will require permanent institutional attention.

For the purpose of promoting efficiency in the conduct of these institutions, two things appear to me to be advisable.

1. In co-operation with the administration of the institution, there ought to be a committee of public-spirited citizens who would be interested and able to act as interpreters of the methods and policies of the institutional management. At Oak Forest about fifteen years ago we had such a committee. It was headed by the late Dr. Theodore B. Sachs, the eminent specialist on tuberculosis. The care of the tubercular patients at Oak Forest was on a dreadfully low level. There was only one trained nurse for three hundred patients, though of course, there were attendants. The laboratory consisted of one microscope. Dr. Sachs' committee undertook to raise the standard and provide for trained nurses. It required an extra appropriation of some $50,000. The committee labored with the members of the finance committee of the county board to obtain this extra money. It required meeting after meeting and in the end it looked as if the Committee would fail. In the final crisis when the last decision seemed to close any hope of the additional money Dr. Sachs turned to the committee and said: "We will not give up, we will do as the Americans say—[he could not for the moment think of the western expression] 'we will not die in bed—we will die with our boots on.'" He got the appropriation.

2. What these institutions need more than anything else is the service of trained social workers. These social workers would know

the needs of the inmates at first hand and would be able to serve them in ways that are unknown to the untrained attendants of these institutions. Some of these attendants and supervisors are devoted and helpful, but they have not the background or training that enables them to seize upon unrecognized factors in the inmate's history that may lead to a recovery of his independent status. The work of a body of trained workers would build up in time a record of approved information and experience that would reveal the needs, possibilities, and limitations of the institutions. I believe that the expense of providing this kind of trained personal service would be more than met by economies they would promote and would make the ministry of the institution more effective, considerate, and merciful.

EDNA L. FOLEY
Superintendent of Visiting Nurse Association of Chicago

Tonight we have failed to consider one aspect of the care of the aged, which seems important in the well-rounded family life, and that is the cultural aspects of the presence in the home of a grandparent or of grandparents. In city apartments, grandparents may be more in the way than they are in city tenements, but not every family wants to get rid of old parents. The happiest memories of a good many childhoods are days or hours spent with grandparents.

A big city organization like a Visiting Nurse Association finds that old people fall into several groups. There are those for whom there is no place in the house, even in a well-to-do home. If they cannot be put into a home for the aged, old people are boarded out, for their children do not want them. The boarding home plan, as we have seen it worked on a fairly small scale, is not very successful, for there is very little money to be made in boarding elderly people. Naturally the homes that take in the boarders wish some profit. Children who try this plan seldom can or will meet the expense, and the old parent is shunted from one private home to another.

A second group of aged people are a real burden in the home, taking space and food and attention that rightly belongs to a younger generation. Even so small a pension as $1.00 a day would help these people pay their way. If the financial tension were relieved, the burden would be less obvious. Over and over again we have found the small Civil War pension just enough to keep the aged dependent in the family from being a real source of anxiety as well as of expense.

Then there is the third group whose natural place (as Mr. Davis has said) is in the home of their children or in a tiny apartment near their children. These old people perform household tasks that keep them happily occupied. They help with the children. They are consulted about family problems. Their children would make any sacrifice before putting their parents "on the town." In homes where this good will prevails, little children get a great deal from their contact with older people.

People in America never used to look upon the older members of their families as burdens. The attitude of certain peasant groups toward elderly relatives, who worked hard in the fields in the summer and begged from door to door in the winter, is to be avoided as well as deplored.

Children have a right to grandparents. It is up to the parent group to see that the happiness of the young is not destroyed by the presence of old people and that the comfort and contentment of old people is not too greatly interfered with by petty annoyances which can be avoided if the in-between age has a proper respect for the rights of both age and youth.

FRANK Z. GLICK

Executive Secretary, Illinois Board of Public Welfare Commissioners

Mr. Chairman, after the brilliant oral thinking presented by the speakers tonight, it would seem presumptuous for me to try to add anything on the subject that they have covered.

With regard to Mr. Cosgrove's review of the program on the Home for Aged Dependents in New York City, I was especially interested in his statement that five social case workers are now employed there. The potential value of social case workers in the institution for care of the aged, in enhancing the lives of the residents and in making adjustments for some of them on the outside, has not yet been fully realized.

The report by Miss Parker on the survey made of private homes for the aged by the United States Census Bureau was especially interesting to me because we have recently made, under the auspices of the Council of Social Agencies, a similar study of forty-two private homes for the aged in metropolitan Chicago. Our study referred particularly to the intake work of these institutions, going into some detail on the investigation work they do with applicants. The eligibility requirements as we found them in this group of homes were substantially the same as those reported by Miss Parker.

The papers presented by Dr. Boas and Dr. Davis tonight have shown that, in that large group of dependent old folks who are chronically or acutely ill, a group which we have been content to think of and deal with as one large but uncomplicated mass, there is a complexity of smaller groups presenting diverse medical diagnoses and diverse needs for care. It will be a long time before the different types of hospitals and institutions are developed to care adequately for these old folks, but it is gratifying to see that we are at least beginning to discern the problem.

At this morning's session of the conference, there was, very apparently, a conflict between those interested in institutional care for the aged and those interested in public subsidy plans. This conflict, it seems to me, is more apparent than real. Our case work with dependent old people, during the past year at the Council of Social Agencies, has shown us that their needs are diverse, that for some institutional care is most advisable and for others support in their own homes would be the best plan. For adequate care we need various kinds of resources. In the future as these resources are made available, the services of case workers to dependent old folks will be more and more in demand. The case workers' job will be to individualize each case, not only at the onset of dependency, but throughout the dependency in order that each case will at all times be utilizing the most advisable resource that is available for its care.

PUBLIC OUTDOOR RELIEF AND THE CARE
OF THE AGED IN MASSACHUSETTS

FRANCIS BARDWELL

Massachusetts Department of Public Welfare, Boston

The Massachusetts system of poor relief was primarily based on the old English poor law, which became operative in England just prior to the beginning of the seventeenth century. This law was fairly started in the running by the time Plymouth was founded, and it was natural that the first colonists in New England should follow it.

It was parish relief. The early settlers advocated and believed in the union of church and state. In fact, the early church came before the state. Later, when the town was the unit of government and religion was not the primary factor, parish relief became town relief, the use of the county as a unit never coming into the picture.

The parish system had its foundation as to the financial responsibility for the dependent person in the settlement or domicile of the individual. This, today, is fundamental.

The title of the dispensing officer was "overseer of the poor." This survived until within a few years when the legal change to "member of the board of public welfare" supplanted it.

The founders of Massachusetts, both the Pilgrim of Plymouth and the Puritan of Salem and Boston, had optimistically planned colonies free from dependents. The example of the poverty-stricken England of that era, where beggary and want were rife and dire need laid a heavy hand upon the inhabitants, must have pointed a terrible example of the misery of the poor and influenced the colonists to frame laws and make every endeavor to avoid the calamity which had so burdened the mother-country. These colonists frowned upon the detached spinster or bachelor; the family must be the unit; and into some family must go these detached individuals. To preserve their independence and prevent dependent people from settling within townships already established, they enacted the law which provided for warning out of town of all who were not desirable

54

or later might prove a charge on the community. And yet, with all these precautions and the desire to build a country without dependents, Boston erected its first almshouse just thirty-two years after its foundation. The mother-country early began sending across undesirables for its colonies overseas to care for. They early indentured dependent children as apprentices, under the supervision of the overseers of the poor, deeming it wise that all boys should learn a trade and all girls be skilled in the domestic arts. This, I feel, was the beginning of the placing-out system, which has probably proved its wisdom most proficiently in Massachusetts, above the other states.

Not until the middle of the nineteenth century, however, did the state, as a supervising body and as a builder of needed public institutions for a definite welfare program, come onto the stage. Prior to this, it had merely been an auditing and disbursing agent for those dependent cases not settled in any municipality. But with the coming of a horde of emigrants, mostly of English, Irish, and Scotch blood, whose dependents swamped the local municipal boards of charity, legislation was necessary and an Alien Commission was formed. This progressed through various vicissitudes, such as a joint Board of Health, Lunacy, and Charity and other titles until we have the present-day Department of Public Welfare. At first the state's supervision of municipal relief was negligible, confronted always by that Yankee independence that ever blocked a central controlling body. In truth, it is this factor that makes the status of the State Department of Public Welfare a supervising and not a controlling body in most of its functions, an educational and not a dominant board. You will take note that at no time in the history of the State Board was the problem of correction linked up with the duties of this department. The poor and the criminal in Massachusetts have always been handled by distinctly different boards.

Always, however, there have been the two classifications of dependents: the town case and the unsettled or state case. But both classes are under the direct care of the authorities of the town of residence, and the state supervises all and pays for the unsettled. There has always been outdoor relief or what is gradually being known as aid to persons in their homes in Massachusetts. Little by little we are becoming educated to the differences between the institutional and non-institutional case. To the aged dependent the understanding of this vital policy by the authorities and the good which follows intelligent placing have made their declining years happier.

Because the state is financially responsible for a certain number of dependent people (the unsettled cases) and has supervision not only over these but over others who fall into the class of settled cases, it has a broad field of work, where it can gradually define policies and lead the municipal boards in their desire to do efficient work. It is through this means that higher standards of care are given and proper placing is carried out. For as the state cases live, so the local cases demand their living. To make this standard assured to all, the state is obliged to visit every person aided by municipal or local relief outside of their own home. As long as the ideals of the State Department are on a high plane and a program of constructive progress is to the fore, advancement is bound to be made.

Perhaps the hardest fight to obtain this end started in 1908 in a movement to do away with the set sum of $2.00 a week in summer and $3.00 a week in winter to each unsettled family. This was an inelastic standard, pitifully small, and was to my mind one of the major causes of various families or tribes, as they became known, becoming hereditary paupers. For, as the state standard was, so became the average municipal or local standard and particularly between towns—and the poor suffered. In 1908, to suggest a standard carrying adequate relief seemed a prediction of financial calamity. But in 1912 such a law was passed, and the State Department began to work with social intelligence and municipalities followed suit.

Can it be called social work when the same financial relief is given to the family of nine as the family of two or three? This is not social work at all; investigation in such cases is wasted time. For the underlying principle of social work is proper investigation to determine the need, to care adequately for that need with a view, in the average family case, of future rehabilitation.

This foreword seemed necessary if we are to understand the method in vogue in Massachusetts for the relief of dependent aged people. The machinery is not complicated. The State Department of Public Welfare, a supervising board, actual relief given by the municipality of the client's place of abode, with financial assistance ultimately paid by the client's place of settlement. Visitation is made by the state to all settled, detached cases and *all* unsettled cases. Under such a system the state wields a tremendous educational influence. And while the effects come slowly, they are permanent and finally become the real standard of relief.

At the present stage, it is foolish to talk of eliminating the almshouse, unless some equivalent system of care for certain types of institutional dependents can be brought forward. But it is wiser to change the almshouse to suit the needs of what we are getting to recognize as the present class which needs this kind of institutional care. At present only 6 per cent of the total dependent population of Massachusetts is housed in almshouses or, as we are pleased to call them, infirmaries. While the population of the state has grown and the number of dependents has also increased, the infirmary population has remained fairly level. It has taken many years to accomplish this elimination.

With us a line of division has been drawn between the institutional and non-institutional case. The standard is simple and is based on common sense and provided, as is the case with us, funds are available for adequate aid to clients in their homes.

Institutional cases are those:

1. Needing hospitalization either because of physical or mental illness.
2. Needing mild custodial care.
3. Incompatible of disposition—hence impossible to place properly at reasonable cost.
4. Desiring to live in a home with other people rather than endure loneliness.

Of these classes, by far the greater number are found among those suffering from chronic or incurable disease, old men and old women who need nursing care. But because the usual trend in our hospitals is against many of such patients and a place must be made for them, we are little by little converting portions of various infirmaries into wards for chronic patients, and when new construction is contemplated urging that it be to serve this purpose. Last year in Massachusetts, wards, totaling in all more than 100 beds, were constructed in three of the infirmaries in smaller cities, one new institution on hospital lines for 200 patients was built, and another for 120 is in process of construction; in the latter all rooms for patients are on the ground floor. Give us ten years more to carry out this program, and all our infirmaries will be such in fact as well as name. This change seems of the most vital importance in considering a complete plan for the care of old people. We are trying to make these hospitals for chronics prove a help to the near-dependent as well as the patient under public aid, and so receive at a minimum cost such cases as cannot be placed, because of the nature of their disease, in the general hospitals. This feature will in time, I think, sweep away the old "poorhouse" prejudice as the infirmary is growing into a municipal hospital for the care of patients suffering from chronic or incurable disease. And because there are so few terminal hospitals, it is bound to be a successful rearrangement. This lack of terminal hospitals is not confined to Massachusetts; it is noted in every state in the union.

I feel perhaps as you do relative to statistics; there can be too many of them and their significance can be misconstrued, but while we hear so much of the dependent aged it is interesting to note first that only about 10 per cent of all public dependents in Massachusetts are over sixty years of age. If we made it sixty-five years of age, the percentage would be materially reduced. It is, therefore, this 10 per cent, or some 14,000 people, in whom we are interested. Why make the age sixty? Is sixty the beginning of old age? There are several definitions of when old age begins. One of my infirmary friends was a man who lived to be nearly one hundred and one years old. He was alert both mentally and physically. It was a pleasure to talk with him, and from him I got his reaction concerning the advancing years. He said he supposed that he really noticed he was getting old about the time he was sixty-five because,

At that age we ceased to hurry; at seventy we discovered sunshine and lingered in it; at seventy-five, we are fussy; at eighty, we demand; at eighty-five, we no longer demand, we have become a person who views the procession apart from it; at ninety, we wait apprehensively and expectantly; at one hundred, we have a celebration and are congratulated; and from then on, the world seems to begrudge us our living.

As old age is considered a disease, the age at which it fastens itself upon the average person varies, but in all honesty we cannot place it below sixty. While the population of the state from 1901 to 1923 has increased 40 per cent, during the same period the number of municipal almshouses has dropped from 221 to 138 and the population of these from 4,561, on day of inspection, to 3,822. This seems conclusive that, with the ratio of public dependence following the trend of population, institutional residence for the dependent poor is materially decreasing. The answer is intelligent outdoor relief and the proper standardization of the institution case. Furthermore, if a pension of a dollar a day was granted, it would only be applicable to a small percentage of almshouse inmates as classified by the present standard; and because the major cause of old age dependence is illness, that factor so destructive to the pocketbook of the aged person. And, now, why have we come here to discuss the care of the dependent aged? A quarter of a century ago most men interested in the care of this class of our citizens felt that providing shelter in an institution was all that could be done. Meanwhile, the expectation of life has stretched farther along toward the century mark—people are younger at seventy than they were twenty years ago at fifty-five. We have done so much for child welfare, so much for the family, so much for the mental defective, for the blind; and then it dawned on us that because of modern industrial conditions humanity is scrapped about ten or fifteen years earlier than it used to be. And as a result, any worker with graying hair who is out of a job stays out of a job. This is one of the boomerangs in our workmen's compensation bill.

Did you ever divide life as follows:

From twenty to forty-five, the generous earning and generous spending years.
From forty-five to sixty, the working and saving years.
From sixty to the end, the spending years.

And, if the working and saving years, from forty-five to sixty, are not productive, dependence comes before sixty-five.

I have come to feel that proper care of old people should embrace the element of happiness, and that in considering the welfare of old people their happiness must be given due consideration. In the majority of cases, old people desire to continue on in their own home. If they are enjoying normal health this can be done. But the tragedy comes if removal for their own sake is necessary. It is the detached case, the old man or the old woman living alone in a home, where many things may happen, that is a problem. In such a case solicitude of considerate neighbors, or supervision and visitation by a church worker, are of material benefit to the client and a great assistance to the local board. You see, in a lot of our cases we never hesitate to call upon the workers of the private agencies, and gradually the old wall between public and private is being broken down. In this respect there is a marked difference between the conditions of the city and rural poor. This problem of dependent old age is really a city problem. Old people are so much better off in the country town—where neighborliness takes the place of social service. It is possible to get an old person comfortably boarded in the country at a reasonable price; it is not such an easy matter to secure a home in a city, where the dollar value is vastly different. But it is always hard to board elderly people—people are willing to take children and in some instances this means more care—at a less price.

And now you are interested in prices—what is a reasonable price? The cheapest rate in a home maintained to care for aged people is $8.00 a week, and from there the price soars to the exclusive home that charges $75.00 a week even. It is obligatory, when funds come from the public treasury, to get board as reasonably as possible. We have hundreds of cases, both state and municipal, in which aged people are boarded with relatives or friends as low as $4.00 a week. Usually this is in cases in which the client can do a little. You doubtless realize that the reason we have twice as many men as women in our almshouses is because an elderly woman is of economic value in the home, and especially in that home with children when both parents work. The dependent or near dependent woman has a greater opportunity than the man, and this is as it should be.

And again as to prices paid. One municipality in Massachusetts, which has a splendid infirmary, is boarding four old ladies in a selected home and paying $12.00 a week for three of them and $15.00 for the other. Why? If they were in the infirmary, they would each have a separate room, each be permitted to furnish it with their own things, and would enjoy good food well cooked, and would be under the charge of a competent and kindly matron used to old people. The answer is that each one of these old ladies has seen better days; in their youth they have been social somebodies in the town, and the community would not approve of their being placed in the infirmary. Could this community interest happen under the county system of public relief?

Then, too, in one of the Berkshire towns which has no infirmary, twelve old people were boarded in homes. The boarding standard was the standard of the overseer, a plain, kindly carpenter who placed these people. I rather doubt if twelve such homes could have been picked in another town in Massachusetts. And the little things considered—nearness to the church for those who went to the church, and not too far from a particular friend, and a home with children for a child-hungry spinster of seventy; it was the little things that made these people happy.

There is always the other side of the picture. I once visited sixty-six boarded-out cases in small hill towns. All types and conditions of men and women—mostly over sixty—some in homes of relatives, some in farmhouses, village homes. Nearly one-half I placed anew, and some of these I got into a nearby infirmary for hospital care. Many of them sad cases of neglect, and some poorly placed through niggardliness. Relatives, I found, were just as disinterested as strangers. It was a test-out of the principle of state supervision and proved the wisdom of the method. These changes were not forced, no legal power rests with the state save when gross neglect is proved. I found no serious opposition on the part of the overseers and in most cases a desire to co-operate for the welfare of the client.

So I feel there must be state supervision, provided that supervision is kindly, helpful, educational, with only the proper placing of the client in view.

Are homes with relatives desirable? The state never boards children with relatives. In the matter of old people, there must be good investigation; sometimes relatives are willing, but the client objects. In such cases the home should be passed. We are placing the client where the client's happiness is an important consideration. But if the client desires to go to relatives it is probable that the price paid will be less than if a regular boarding home is chosen.

I have met many men and women, but mostly women, who prefer the public home to living with their children. But by law the obligation to support is placed upon the child or grandchild, provided the child or grandchild is financially able to contribute to the support; ability to do so is determined by the court. Most of these cases never get as far as the court. The son or his wife dreads the effects on the family's social standing too much to risk a court summons.

In the matter of state supervision, two matters closely allied in the care of old people are responsibilities of the Welfare Department. The first of these is in its investigation and final granting of charters to charitable corporations, and the second is the licensing and supervision of boarding homes for aged people. Over 250 million dollars is invested in these private charitable corporations, and over 44 million dollars is expended yearly against about 11 million by public relief. Of interest to us is the fact that there are 114 incorporated homes for the aged, which care for about 3,000 persons sixty-five years of age and over. And these are permanent as against an almshouse population totaling over 7,000 in individual cases, but as of residence about 3,500.

You must realize that this care by private agencies takes a big burden from the taxpayer and throws it onto the voluntary contributions of the philanthropic. For charitable purposes in Massachusetts, aside from contribution of the churches and fraternal orders and the like, 55 million is spent for a population estimated at 4 million. Is it any wonder we look askance at an impending pension and its additional sum placed anywhere from 6 to 20 millions? The problem is not of more money, but the judicial expenditure of what already exists.

These incorporated homes for the aged are hemmed about by certain restrictions—racial, religious, geographical, etc. They take for the most part the superior type of dependent from the large municipalities. They charge a nominal entrance fee, and all have long waiting lists. In conjunction, several have out-patient departments, a most wise measure which minimizes the agony of a dwindling entrance fee and a fading possibility of being taken care of. The great need in all these homes is an infirmary to care for the chronic sick. And sometime I hope these homes may get together and provide a temporary home for applicants, thus conserving the entrance fee and forestalling the almshouse. The second matter is the licensing of boarding homes for aged people under a law passed in May last year. Under statute this matter was given to the Department of Public Welfare to investigate, make regulations, and issue licenses. The law is broad enough to allow supervision, and licenses may be revoked by the State Department. Certain physical conditions of the buildings used are carefully considered, as, for instance, if patients occupy rooms above the ground floor, there must be two exits to the ground. Bed and wheel chair cases are by preference entitled to ground floor rooms and cannot be housed above the second floor. As to rooms, food, care, and the like, consideration is taken of the price paid. These prices start at $8.00 a week and go up to $75.00. Any person boarding more than two people who are upward of sixty comes under the law.

Formerly it has been customary for certain people to contract for a stated amount, say from $1,000 to $3,000, to give life care to an aged person. This was decidedly hazardous for the aged client. The state now requires a bond and of sufficient amount so that an annuity can be purchased if the contract is broken. This has had the desired effect; it has stopped the practice completely.

About 125 licenses have been granted to date. It is probable that 300 such homes exist in Massachusetts. Allied with this, the state has an index of homes based on prices and locations, and already it has proved of benefit to friends and relatives desiring to place patients. By it, the state keeps in closer touch with these licensed homes and is able to arrest trouble at the start.

A word about annuities. Why are annuities so seldom taken in this country? Why is savings bank insurance so seldom used? Is it the American spirit of procrastination? Initial payment of $5.00 at twenty-five years, and $1.00 per week until sixty-five, would yield a life annuity of $550, or cash $4,588.20, and the client has been insured for from $1000 the first year to $5,380 at sixty-five.

I have seen a number of aged women having in savings banks

sums from $5,000 to $10,000, drawing $4\frac{1}{2}$ per cent who, if they bought an annuity at sixty-five with the money, could enjoy from $550 to $1000 a year. Why won't they do it? Relatives—relatives who don't want them won't keep them, but expect the savings.

To sum up, we want:

a) Good investigation and intelligent placement.

b) To separate the institution and non-institution cases.

c) To provide more hospitals for the chronic sick at minimum price.

d) Painstaking supervision by state and local boards.

e) Friendly visitation.

f) The moral support of the private charitable agencies, and possible financial help to tide over special cases.

g) Responsible visitors to assist and advise the *near* dependent.

In a program of this kind, the state must take the initiative.

THE RELATION OF THE FAMILY SERVICE
AGENCY TO THE CARE OF THE AGED

H. L. LURIE

Superintendent, Jewish Social Service Bureau, Chicago

Organized philanthropic care of the dependent aged has assumed two general aspects of service. These may be termed institutional or domiciliary care, and case work service. The family agency, as a general case-working organization dealing with the problems of individual adjustment, has been concerned largely with the adjustment of aged persons as one among many groups of individual and family situations.

The important phases of case work consist of the supplying of income to aged individuals, permitting them to continue living in the community, and assisting in the program of the individual, with or without financial relief, in order to improve his circumstances and to bring about a more desirable adjustment. An understanding, therefore, of the needs of social service for the aged persons, requires evaluation of the resources, facilities, and methods of adjustment which social agencies bring to this problem.

The family agency may be considered, therefore, as having at its disposal, case work service and financial assistance, or special resources for the aged exclusive of institutional homes for dependent aged. Although the individual receiving institutional care might also benefit from individualized attention, and case work service is not out of place in the institutional program, the present discussion will relate itself to the non-institutional forms of case work service.

If there is any contribution which the case worker may make to the planning of programs for the care of the aged, it lies in the fact that the emphasis of case work is placed upon individualizing the problem of the aged, and in the development of a flexible program which attempts to deal with the many variations to be found in the problems and adjustments required by this as by other groups of persons in need. Lack of direct contact tends to build up an abstract, and frequently an unreal, concept of the problems of a group and of the solutions required, so that general programs suggested are frequently limited in perspective, and emphasize a single method of solution. To the family agency which deals with the problem of the individual, the concept of the aged as a uniform group of dependents tends to break down. Instead, the aged take on the vivid colors of personalities, and present themselves as affected by varied problems and require varied services for their solution.

Not all of the aged persons outside of the public and private charitable institutions are in need of organized forms of service. A number of such persons are making satisfactory adjustments in their own communities either because of normal sources of income, from property, or through their own earnings from gainful occupations. Others are independent of social agencies because they are members of self-maintaining family groups and are accepted in such groups because of their value in the home, or because of strong emotional attachments upon the part of the family group. The family agency comes into contact with aged persons of this category at the time of economic stress or when new home and family adjustments must be made, or when temporary dislocations or new problems make it necessary for the individual to seek outside advice and assistance. The case work method of dealing with such problems requires a comprehensive study of important social and personal factors present in any given situation. After such study a more satisfactory adjustment for the individual within the resources of the community or of the agency, and within the possibilities of the individual himself, can be attempted. The general conclusion, which case work agencies have drawn from their many years of work with individual problems, is that there is a wide range of situations and also a wide range in the factors of adjustment which can be made available. Social agencies find that in the individual himself who has come to the attention of the agency there may be potential resources which, if properly developed, assist the individual to make a better adjustment. There are, for example, the possibilities of an earning capacity not yet exhausted. There are many individuals who apply to social agencies beyond the chronological age of sixty-five, who have not necessarily reached the stage where complete or partial self-support must be entirely ruled out. There are special kinds of employment which may be secured, suitable for the aged person. Such employment constitutes a type of adjustment which the individual himself frequently prefers. Many of the so-called "aged" present no outstanding health difficulties nor work limitations for the less strenuous or sedentary occupations. Even where ill health is involved, illness may be temporary, and proper medical service given at the appropriate time results in an improvement sufficient for a normal participation in occupational life. There are, on the other hand, many individuals for whom illness constitutes the cause of dependency, and represents the beginning of chronic disabilities and ailments which make normal occupational adjustment difficult, if not impossible.

There are also present, in many instances of aged dependents, the normal and natural social resources of the individual. Few aged persons are socially isolated. One has not lived for sixty-five or seventy years or longer without having established for himself a number of natural contacts and associations. There are, first, the immediate families of the aged individual, the original kinship group of the individual, and the group which he has acquired through marriage. There are possibilities of collateral relatives for the aged person who has not married, or if married, has no living children. There are, in addition, acquaintances, members of fraternal organizations, interested neighbors and friends, former employers and work associates. These are resources and natural associations of the individual that are not necessarily lost or non-existent at the time the individual makes his application to a social agency for assistance. The social worker can, upon occasion, bring about a better relationship of the client to these other persons in his environment, frequently better than the individual himself, unaided. Among former employers, church and fraternal affiliations, as well as among close relatives and friends, occasional adjustments are possible which may be more satisfactory to the client than philanthropic aid. It is within these associations that the life of the individual previously revolved, and some of them are capable of being restored so that they constitute a desirable adjustment for the client.

The customary means of adjustment for the aged person within his own social setting are, however, frequently unavailable or do not respond to case work service. There is need of organizing new resources, financial and otherwise, for the aged person. The social agencies have, therefore, found it necessary to develop special facilities for aged persons. Temporary financial assistance may be necessary to tide over the individual for a period of weeks or months until such time as a more permanent plan can be worked out. Special medical facilities, free clinical and hospital service for acute or temporary illness, visiting nursing service, temporary loans, legal aid, and other services are required and in some communities can be made available to aged persons. Other special resources for the care of the aged include sheltered industries, such as the Workshops for the Aged of the New York Association for Improving the Condition of the Poor. In other cases sheltered workshops which deal with a variety of handicapped persons, such as the Industrial Workshops of Chicago, have opportunities for a limited number of aged persons. Some organizations make a special effort in the direction of finding suitable private homes and residences for aged persons who can adjust themselves either by their own efforts, or with the organized assistance of relatives or friends, or with partial and complete support through philanthropic sources. Some progress is being made in this direction as an alternative to the institutional home for aged persons.

We have little means for knowing how large a proportion of individuals, who are not properly adjusted in their own social setting and might be benefited by service, actually apply for the services which the social agencies are able to offer. In addition to the persons who have come to them for assistance there are others in the community who, unaided by philanthropic agencies, are making a totally unsatisfactory or a partially unsatisfactory adjustment. The resources of the local agency, its reputation in the community, the attitude current in the community in general and in the racial or cultural groups toward applying and receiving assistance from particular organizations, the standards of service and the kinds of resources which are available, are no doubt factors influencing the extent of case work service.

In addition to the variations which exist between social agencies, there are differences of circumstances under which applications to such agencies take place. The question, "Under what circumstances will a dependent aged person, who has self-supporting children, seek the assistance of a community agency," has many answers. In the experience of our own organization, the reasons for the application depend upon economic, psychological, and health factors. Economic factors are important and varied. There are self-supporting children of aged persons who even under meager living conditions will continue to maintain aged relatives, and will not seek special community aid for one considered a regular member of their family group. On the other hand, lack of a satisfactory income for the family group is frequently the reason that children urge, or the aged person himself prefers, to seek outside aid. As a contrast to this type, there are self-supporting children who possess reasonably comfortable incomes and decent standards of living, who feel themselves unable or unwilling to extend the family income to cover the needs of the aged member of their group. Social agencies are familiar with applications for relief or institutional care from aged persons in the middle-class economic groups, particularly from those groups who strain to maintain a higher standard of living. It might be said in these situations that application for community assistance is made not because of the economic needs of the family group but on account of the attitude of the family toward their standard of living as affected by an additional dependent. Psychological and affectional factors in these situations are therefore important. Between the family group that will maintain an economic struggle in order to continue responsibility for an aged dependent, and the family group under comfortable economic circumstances who will readily shift the burden of responsibility to a public or private institution that offers care to aged persons, there is a wide gamut of social attitudes.

Personality factors are frequently involved in the attitudes of self-supporting children who seek community assistance for an aged dependent. These can only be understood when the entire psychological and social history of the family is known. There are parents who have no logical reason, aside from custom, for expecting the filial obligations of their children when old age comes upon them. There are aged persons who have been indifferent and unsatisfactory parents, individuals, who may have deserted the children in the past, have exploited or thwarted the development of their children. There are, in addition, more subtle situations involved in antagonism between parent and child, possibly related to early abnormal emotional situations such as those found by mental-hygiene clinics as factors in behavior maladjustments of young children. Psychological factors of this type vary from former experiences of oversolicitude of parents and jealousy and rivalry in the family group, to actual neglect and indifference.

Changing cultural and social factors in the life-history of parents and children may offer another explanation for the dissolving of familial ties and responsibilities. Particularly among immigrant groups cultural adjustments proceed at a different pace between the two generations. The immigrant parents may, for a time, be satisfactorily adjusted with their children during the early years of residence in a new country. With continued residence, however, the cultural life of the children alters radically, influencing religious belief and social status, until finally the aged person finds himself estranged from the life to which the children are aspiring. Application for the community care of an aged parent comes frequently from children who are moving up the social and economic scale, as indicated by transfer of residence from an area of immigrant settlement to the newer and more favorably situated areas of the urban locality. In our own organization we find, for example, that, when the adult children who have been caring for dependent aged move from the old lower west side to a newer and more Americanized portion of the city, neither the children nor the parents feel comfortable in the new area with the aged parent as a member of the family group. The new neighborhood, with its different standards of habits and manners, the changed religious atmosphere of the home, and the absence of nearby religious institutions affect the family situation. Aged persons begin to feel the difference in taste, in habit, in outlook upon life which separates them from their children, and seek for solution through the community agencies which function for the benefit of persons of their ideas and temperaments.

The marriage of children introduces into the family group new individuals who intentionally or unconsciously may become the disturbing elements in a family situation which previously offered a satisfactory home for the aged person. A daughter-in-law or a son-in-law, or the grandchildren, so affect and change the home situation that it ceases to be desirable. It is in such instances that lack of resources on the part of the aged person or the additional burden of caring for him, or the struggle to adjust one's viewpoint to the needs and requirements of an aged person, constitute the precipitating factor and bring about the application for care. It may be said that these influences in the home-situation are the stimulating agents in bringing about an unsatisfactory adjustment in the home. Whether the unhappiness caused in such instances will result in the use of community resources depends largely upon the nature and standards of the alternative ways of caring for aged persons. When almshouses are inadequate and disagreeable, there will be hesitation in referring aged dependents to their care. Similarly, if the private home for the aged is uncomfortable and meager, there will be greater hesitation displayed in referring a dependent relative. If the acceptance of public outdoor relief or private aid carries with it the stigma of a grudging assistance, or is inadequate in character, the number of applicants for such assistance will be affected. On the other hand, it is logical to suppose, from our present experience, that the aged person, as well as his self-supporting children, seem to be more willing to consider philanthropic aid when it consists of desirable and adequate homes for aged persons, established for the essential needs and comfort of the aged person, and considered, in spite of philanthropic support, as available to aged persons eligible for such care upon the basis of fraternal affiliations, nationality, or religion.

We may offer the general conclusion, from the experience of case work agencies, that improvement in resources available to aged persons, and changes in the philosophy underlying the offer of service for the aged, whether it be that of an institutional home and public subsidy, or a private individual grant, will radically affect the extent to which aged persons, not entirely supported through their own funds and resources, seek the assistance which the community has to offer.

It is important that we set forth clearly the values and the deficiencies in the present program of case work service to the aged. Insistence upon the development of the natural resources of the individual, the conservation and enhancement of the normal responsibilities of family, employers, and of associational groups, serves as the mainstay for the present program. Of greater importance, perhaps, and offering justification for the continuance of case work effort as an integral part of any new plan for the care of the dependent aged, is that case work service makes possible the discovery of the factors involved in each particular situation. The understanding of the problems of individual personality, of health, and of psychological maladjustment, cannot fail but to be helpful in the assistance to be rendered to the aged person. Such study helps to place the emphasis of care upon the normal aspects of life of the individual. Case work emphasizes the desirability to the able-bodied aged person, of normal interests and occupations. It is recognized that the aged person presents the need for attention to health matters. The case work program, to some extent, focuses upon the building-up of special services to meet the needs of aged persons. It aims to develop an appreciation of the values of normal community life for dependents; the value in the retention of old associates, family friends; and the desirability of considering an aged person not as a special type, but as a person sharing in normal community life. Such values have stimulated, to a small extent, the development of programs of relief by philanthropic agencies. A recent example is the establishment of the Hannan Memorial Home, and the John Scudder Trust for Old People, which has been organized in Detroit and offers varied programs of assistance and relief to aged persons.

While careful accounting of the relative costs of administration of institutional homes as compared with outdoor relief has not been made, there is some possibility that the cost of service to aged persons in their own homes or in private family homes in the community may be more economical than institutional service. This may depend upon a greater flexibility in the outdoor methods of care, greater emphasis upon the contributions which the relatives make to such programs, or upon the fact that an individual supported in the community has fewer limitations in adding to his own maintenance than does the person housed in an institutional group. An individual receiving outdoor relief may, after a short period, be able to make an adjustment on his own initiative, whereas an individual accepted by an institution may be more apt to consider such acceptance as final and permanent. Relatives who may be unable to support an aged person entirely, may find that with a partial subsidy the aged person no longer imposes a financial burden upon the family group. They may, however, be unable, even with the best of intentions, to contribute to an institution for the care of the aged. It is in such economies that the outdoor method of relief of the aged, the so-called "pension" plan, may be able to function for the welfare of the aged at a smaller individual cost than that necessitated by fixed and permanent institutions.

There are, however, very important and very serious limitations at the present time to the program of care of the aged developed by case-working organizations. First, and most important, are the geographical limitations of the case work agencies of high standards which I have had in mind in this discussion. Acceptable standards of service exist sporadically in the large centers of population, and only for such parts of the urban population as have developed satisfactory economic and cultural standards. For many groups in large cities, in the smaller towns, and in the open country, little organized case work exists, and limited attention is given to the problems of the aged.

An equally important limitation lies in the fact that there exist in few places definite and clear-cut policies as to whether the institution or home for the aged or outdoor relief shall be the basis of care. The family agency is concerned not only with the aged but with many other problems of individual maladjustment; unemployment, chronic illness, disorganized children, disorganized families, mental deficients. With such general responsibilities, resources are insufficient for developing a systematic and satisfactory program for the care of the aged. With the varieties of demands upon the family agency, the problem of child welfare in the younger families may loom as a more important consideration. With these limitations the policy is frequently established, even in case work organizations of professional quality and standards, that the aged person needing continued financial assistance is to be sent to the almshouse or to the old people's home. On this account private family agencies, as well as public welfare departments, have done very little in the development of relief plans for aged persons. Philanthropic contributions for this particular problem are more apt to be bestowed upon established homes and institutions. Increased resources available for outdoor relief of the aged through private or public case work agencies may be developed. However, it is not likely that such contributions will be adequate to the needs of the aged unless there is definite organization for this purpose. Such organization is suggested in proposed legislation, which extends the availability of outdoor relief to aged persons, and constitutes statutory authority for the improvement of methods of outdoor relief, and authorizes the increase of relief funds.

Increase in the amount, or extending the conditions under which outdoor relief may be given to aged persons, may serve to limit the availability of natural resources of the family or associational group for the dependent aged. Changing urban conditions, particularly changes in the economic conditions and availability of employment for aged persons, will undoubtedly hasten the necessity for increased community responsibility for the aged. Even though the new forms of relief may be called upon to serve aged persons now cared for by their own family groups, such extension is desirable rather than otherwise. The generous impulse of the natural family and associational groups to which the aged person belongs, cannot be stretched beyond the point of voluntary care. Compulsion exercised upon relatives, former employers, and church groups, due to the lack of alternative solutions, is impermanent and engenders underlying antagonisms and attitudes which are not salutary to the dependent person who is being assisted. Although at the present time many of the adjustments made by case workers are with the individual's own family, they are not wholly satisfactory either to the family or to the aged person. Such arrangements cannot be considered satisfactory merely because some adjustment has been made. Even though the family has assumed the care of the dependent aged, it may have done so because all other avenues of solution have been withheld, or because a psychological attitude has been created which makes it difficult for the family to avail themselves of the inadequate or indifferent resources which do exist.

There is also the factor of irregularity and undependability in the responsibility assumed by privately supported case work organizations. Some years, when economic conditions are satisfactory and other demands for assistance are not excessive, a number of aged persons may be assisted regularly. On the other hand, when economic conditions change, perhaps as a result of an industrial depression, the family agencies are called upon excessively to meet new demands and new problems, and funds for the aged may be curtailed and policies changed, with greater emphasis upon referring aged persons to the institution or to the almshouse ready to receive them.

Another serious obstacle to the development of programs of outdoor relief by case work agencies lies in the fact that traditional attitudes existing in the community, if not in the organization itself, rarely permit the individual to feel that he is receiving assistance of a definite nature to which he can look forward for the remainder of his period of need. There is necessarily involved in all such programs the basic idea that relief is being given by volunteer benevolence rather than as an assured and acceptable method of care to which the individual is morally entitled. Such attitudes are modified by the development of statutory methods of care which are the expression of new social attitudes rather than continuations of the traditional philosophy of poor relief. It is significant to note the extent to which the mothers' pension systems in the United States have developed a newer social philosophy toward dependent mothers, in the minds of the public, among the social workers, as well as in the recipients of aid. Methods of administration and the attitudes developed in the actual performance of social service are important factors in this connection.

A further problem involved in the community care of aged persons, which must be taken into consideration in any revised program of legislation, is to be found in the changing needs of the dependent aged. Outdoor relief may be satisfactory to the individual and to the agency while adjustment in the family home is possible, but becomes entirely unsuitable because of illness, senility, or personality changes.

The agency may find itself unable to continue its program of relief satisfactorily for these reasons, and may find it difficult or impossible to organize a desirable adjustment for the aged person. It becomes increasingly difficult to find a satisfactory institution for an aged person who has become chronically ill or disabled. Hospitals for chronically ill and aged are limited in extent, and the county infirmary or almshouse is frequently considered an undesirable place by the person who has become ill or disabled.

In conclusion, it may be said that case work service for the aged, while limited in scope and extent, has been important in establishing the variety of problems and situations involved in the care of the aged which must be considered in any revised or enlarged program for their care. Case work supplementing an improved system of relief, enlarged medical and institutional resources for the aged who need such forms of care, flexible policies and standards of relief, special medical centers, and specialized institutions, should be integrated into a uniform and well-established program. The efficient use of such integrated programs will depend, to a large extent, upon the intelligent nature of the case work service offered to the clients and applicants of such service. A program for the care of the aged, in addition to offering economic resources for dependents, must offer intelligent service to the aged person along medical, personality, social adjustment, and other needs. The facilities for the care of dependent aged need to be improved at many points.

FACING OLD AGE

ABRAHAM EPSTEIN

Executive Secretary, American Association for Old Age Security, New York City

With the rise in our standards and the diffusion of comfort among the great masses of our people, the question how to remain secure in old age is confronting millions of American men and women today. With Governor Franklin D. Roosevelt, of New York, we are becoming conscious that "no greater tragedy exists in our civilization than the plight of aged, worn-out workers who after a life of ceaseless effort and useful productivity must look forward for their declining years to a dismal poorhouse with the accompanying loss of self-respect and interest in life."

While we are decades behind other industrial nations in our attempt to make this period of life more secure, our backwardness in this respect is not altogether surprising. Our country's industrialization and urbanization, the main factors responsible for the acuteness of the present problem, occurred a good deal later than in the older industrial nations. A leading insurance authority estimated recently that only about 1 per cent of our present industrial establishments are a generation old. Such a basic industry as iron and steel, which was second in value of products in 1919, did not begin on a large scale before the nineties. The United States Steel Corporation did not come into existence before the beginning of this century. The automobile industry, third in the value of products in 1919, is entirely a child of this century. The motion picture industry was unknown 25 years ago; and many of our largest corporations, such as the Ford Company, General Motors, Radio Corporation, and the like, have grown up in the last decade or two. So long as our population remained largely rural and we had an ample supply of free and fertile land, there was no serious problem of old age dependency. In a pioneering country even "Each for himself and the devil take the hindmost" gets accepted as a sound social philosophy. Children or relatives generally took care of the old men and women who fell by the wayside, or these derelicts were thrust into our poorhouses, where they were soon forgotten.

With the rapid expansion and mechanization of our industries, the migration from rural to urban centers, the disappearance of free land, and the shortened working period of life, old age dependency is assuming quite a different aspect today. Poverty in old age can no longer be made impervious by mere hard work, frugality, and good habits. Our future depends altogether upon too many forces beyond our control. The ranks of the destitute aged contain only too frequently the once wealthy and prosperous. One New York Home for the Aged housed among others, an artist, a musician, a broker, an engineer, a teacher, a clergyman, and a lawyer, all of out-standing accomplishments and some of international reputation. The states which have been operating under old age pension laws disclose that no one, no matter what his economic or social status is at a younger age, can be sure of a dignified "sunset of life."

As competitors in the modern industrial system, the aged are faced with innumerable obstacles and with few opportunities of overcoming them. Standardized production has greatly eliminated the need for skill and experience—the sole assets of the older employee under the handicraft system. In a recent article Mr. Henry Ford was quoted as saying that "The man who has never had any experience at all is the best fellow when it comes to fitting him into a new scheme of production. People must never get too much of a habit." The swifter pace required of the modern workman also helps to wear him out at an earlier period. The introduction of new inventions and more specialized machinery generally involves the replacing of men. Since the older workers find it harder to adjust themselves to new processes of work, they are the first to be "let out." The difficulty of finding a job after the prime of life has passed has become proverbial. Many industries now limit the hiring age to forty and thirty-five years.

The conditions found in "Middletown" are typical. Among the males fifteen years of age and over, in the entire city population studied by the Lynds, 12 per cent were between the ages of twenty and twenty-four. However, an investigation of two of the city's leading machine shops showed that the percentage of male workers in this age group was 19 per cent in one and 27 per cent in the other. In the city's male population, 27 per cent were between the ages of forty-five and sixty-four, but in the shops studied only 17 and 12 per cent of the workers were between these ages. The age group sixty-five and over constituted 7 per cent of the total male population in the city, but the shops investigated contained only from 1 to 2 per cent of these older workers.

The 1920 U.S. census data support the "Middletown" findings. These figures show that while the aged are still holding their places among the gainfully employed in agriculture, in the professions, in small businesses, and even in the public service, they are practically eliminated from all the major industrial occupations. Thus 8.08 per cent of aged farmers, or about twice the normal, are still gainfully at work after their sixty-fifth birthday. Among lawyers, judges, and justices more than twice the normal average of aged are still holding their positions. Retail dealers, generally made up of independent small business men, also retain a higher than average percentage in old age. For bankers, brokers, and money-lenders the proportion of those still employed at sixty-five is 5.4 per cent, while the percentage of aged manufacturers and officials still gainfully occupied is considerably higher than the average. But what a different tale is told by the statistics of industrial and mechanical pursuits or of transportation! In these occupations the old seem to have no place, and only from one-fourth to one-fifth of the general average of gainfully occupied aged persons are still working. Less than 2 per cent of miners, clerks, mechanics, moulders, printers, plumbers, etc. are at work after their sixty-fifth year.

While the difficulties of finding a job in middle age and after are increasing, the period of old age itself is growing longer. Through the development of medical science and sanitation, a phenomenal increase in the average span of life has been made possible. As against an average expectancy of life of forty years in 1855, the present life span is fifty-eight years. As a result of this development, the number of aged persons in the United States has been increasing both absolutely and relatively. In 1870 men and women sixty-five years of age and over numbered but little over 1,000,000 and constituted 3 per cent of the population. Today the number of these aged is close to 6,000,000 and they constitute about 5 per cent of the total. At the same time, the earlier possibility of support from children is also diminishing. Families are growing smaller. The city apartment is replacing the old homestead and family ties are weakening. There is no place in the modern apartment for "grandfather's corner."

In addition to the general trends discussed above, there are a number of specific forces that tend to drive thousands of workers toward helplessness in old age. We can mention but a few.

Ill health stands out as the largest single factor of dependency. It is the paramount cause for charitable relief. Every day finds over 2,000,000 ill persons in the United States. Once sickness has set in, the savings of a lifetime may be wiped out soon enough. A prominent woman doctor applied to the Pennsylvania Commission on Old Age Pensions because an illness which overtook her at sixty had eaten up the accumulation of her thirty years' practice and left her penniless at seventy. The annual toll of from 2,500,000 to 3,000,000 industrial accidents occurring in the United States helps further to increase old age destitution.

Unemployment is another devastating factor causing old age poverty. Even in normal times about 10 per cent of our labor supply is unemployed. Due to the constant displacement of workers by machinery and labor-saving devices, the number at present is considerably higher.

Business and banking failures also frequently transform prosperous individuals into paupers and dependents. We hear only of the successful business men. The thousands who fail receive but scant notice in the press. Only those who climb successfully receive public attention, while we forget the many more who are forced down. Recent bank failures in New York brought to light some pitiful cases. The sharp decline in the stock market a short while ago unquestionably augmented the army of aged dependents.

Institutional care, it seems to me, offers no solution of the difficulties of old men and women whose dependency is entirely a result of the inability to participate actively in our industrial world and who are still physically capable of taking care of themselves. That we should provide adequate medical and nursing care for those who are really indigent and unable to obtain this care otherwise goes without saying. But, unfortunately, only in rare instances do our country and township almshouses provide such adequate medical care. Healthy and self-respecting old men and women do not belong in an institution which shelters in its walls the miscellany of unfortunates; the feeble-minded, the epileptics, the crippled, and the imbeciles as well as the retired criminals. Certainly, it is inconceivable that in our present state of development we should still tolerate the daily brutality of separating an old lady from her husband upon their entering the portals of our almshouses after they had lived together for a lifetime and at a time when they need each other most.

The preference of home care as against institutional care seems to be universally acknowledged today. It is the principle underlying our mother's pension legislation which has been found sound and effective. Thirty-eight foreign nations, including virtually every industrial country on earth, have for many decades attempted to solve their problem of old age dependency through a system of state allowances or through the establishment of compulsory insurance plans. At least 650,000,000 people are now protected under such social provisions. These nations have recognized that under modern industrial conditions old age must be made a social responsibility and that the men and women who had given their all in toil and labor are entitled to at least a minimum of comforts when society no longer gives them the opportunity to remain economically independent.

Considerable progress has already been made by the movement for old age security in this country. Since 1914, the legislatures of fourteen states and the territory of Alaska have passed old age pension bills of one type or another. At this moment, old age pension laws are on the statute books of California, Colorado, Kentucky, Maryland, Minnesota, Montana, Nevada, Utah, Wisconsin, Wyoming, and the Territory of Alaska. In the state of Washington a bill passed by the legislature was vetoed by the governor. In Arizona a law adopted in 1914 was declared unconstitutional because of the ambiguity and loose wording of the act. In Pennsylvania, the 1923 Old Age Assistance Act was declared null and void because of certain constitutional limitations. At this time pensions are being paid in

California, Montana, Utah, and Wisconsin. New York is expected to adopt a pension law shortly. (As this goes to press, we are glad to report that pension laws have been adopted in 1930 by the states of New York and Massachusetts. Payments under the New York law began on January 1, 1931, and about 25,000 have already been pensioned. Payments under the Massachusetts law will begin July, 1931. In 1931 pension laws were also enacted in the states of Delaware and Idaho. A number of other states are still expected to join the pension ranks.

It is plain, therefore, that the problems facing the aged today are quite different and more complex than those of a generation or two ago. Innumerable forces beyond the control of the individual contribute to make this period the most insecure in life. The new conditions offer a challenge to our intelligence. To meet them right, they require the formulation of the most socially constructive and statesmanlike programs.

THE OLD AGE SECURITY ACT OF THE
STATE OF NEW YORK[1]

SEABURY C. MASTICK

Senate of the State of New York, Albany

The question of old age security or of old age pensions has béen
before the Legislature of the state of New York, as it has before the
legislatures of many other states, for a number of years. The question in New York came to a head in the session of 1929, when a
full hearing was held on various old age pension bills, a number
of them being based on the so-called "standard plan" proposed by
the Fraternal Order of Eagles and the American Association for
Old Age Security. As a result of this hearing a Legislative Commission of nine members was appointed to "study and investigate
the industrial conditions of aged men and women in order to ascertain and report to the legislature the most practical and efficient
method of providing security against old age want." This Commis-
mission, organized in July, 1929, and with a large staff of research
workers, spent some seven months in an intensive study of conditions in New York, holding public hearings in the principal cities.
The Commission also sent out large numbers of questionnaires and
had the active assistance of many citizens and organizations interested in welfare work. The result of the Commission's deliberations
were embodied in three bills introduced in the Legislature on February 16, 1930. These bills are still in committee awaiting the holding
of a public hearing.

Before entering upon a discussion of the Commission's recommendations, it should be pointed out that the state of New York has
adopted a Public Welfare Law,[2] which repealed all of the previously
existing poor laws dating from 1778 to 1928, inclusive, and setting
up an entirely new basis for public relief and care of the poor. The
title "superintendent of the poor" was changed to "county commissioner of public welfare" or "city commissioner of public welfare,"

[1] This paper was presented by Senator Mastick only a few weeks before the bill
became an act. For an analysis of the Act, see page 132.

[2] *New York Laws* (1929), chap. 565. (See *Social Service Review*, III, 412-21.)

as the case may be, and the title of "overseer of the poor" was changed to "town public welfare officer." Each county in the state was constituted a public welfare district, and certain districts were constituted city public welfare districts. The attempt was made throughout the act to get away from the stigma of pauperism and to place the whole subject of relief on a high plane of social service. It is unnecessary to go into details of the act, but I shall quote Section 77 because it discloses the purpose of the act and indicates the great change in attitude from that existent since Elizabethan times.

Care to be given. It shall be the duty of public welfare officials, insofar as funds are available for that purpose, to provide adequately for those unable to maintain themselves. They shall, whenever possible, administer such care and treatment as may restore such persons to a condition of self-support, and shall further give such service to those liable to become destitute as may prevent the necessity of their becoming public charges.

As far as possible families shall be kept together, and they shall not be separated for reasons of poverty alone. Whenever practicable, relief and service shall be given a poor person in his own home; the commissioner of public welfare may, however, in his discretion, provide relief and care in a boarding home, the home of a relative, a public or private home or institution, or in a hospital.

After much deliberation the Commission came to the conclusion that it was wiser and more practicable to build up old age security on the foundation afforded by the Public Welfare Act than it was to attempt to use or create an entirely new and different agency. The Public Welfare Act went into effect January 1, 1930, and we have therefore as yet no experience from which to deduce its operation. It has been well said that the principles of the act which I have quoted in the foregoing make it possible to care for not only aged citizens but all others in the state needing relief and to do this in their own homes rather than to send them to a county home or poorhouse. The difficulty with the operation of the Public Welfare Act, in our opinion, is that it is not strictly compulsory in character, relief being dependent upon adequate appropriations by the legislative bodies of the counties and the cities. It was thought that to provide definitely for old age security it was necessary to have a compulsory law which would supplement the Public Welfare Act and provide for the aged as a special class. At all points we had in mind the sense of pride inherent in the self-respecting aged poor and endeavored to provide a method of applying for and receiving aid and assistance in a manner which would not bear any stigma.

During its investigations the Commission through one or another of its members visited every county home in the state, observing the character of inmates and the type of care they were receiving. It also made an intensive study in certain typical rural districts and city areas.

As a result of its studies the Commission came to the following conclusions for the reasons stated:

1. Many of the needy aged are not now adequately or properly cared for in the state of New York.

The almshouse is not a satisfactory method of providing relief for all classes of the needy. It is the lineal descent of the workhouses and farms, which were first erected to care for the homeless and unemployed, and not primarily for the sick and the aged who inhabit them today. Investigations made by this and by other legislative commissions have shown that in some of the almshouses there is no segregation of the sick from the able-bodied, or the mentally alert from the feeble-minded. In many instances husband and wife are separated because no provision has been made, or can be made, for keeping them together. Institutions are necessary for certain classes of the poor and for certain of the aged, especially for the sick, but the city and county home should be the last resort for the care of the aged who are normal mentally and physically. In a great many instances, better care and greater comfort can be provided outside of public institutions in the individual's private home.

In many instances the inability of persons over seventy years of age to provide for their own needs is easily determinable as it is caused either by sickness, accident, mental incapacity, or the usual infirmities of old age. Inasmuch as the earning capacity of the aged does not change from day to day or from month to month, the administration of proper relief and care to such persons is a continuous and constant need. For these reasons, assistance to such persons can be considered a different and separate problem from that of needy persons under the age of seventy, who, generally, still have a chance for physical rehabilitation or restoration of earning capacity.

The Commission therefore recommended that needy persons over the age of seventy be considered separately with particular reference to the administration of assistance, relief, and care, and adopted as a vital and fundamental recommendation that the financial responsibility for the relief of such needy aged be not assessed solely upon the public welfare district, whether a county or a city, but that half the responsibility be assumed by the state as a necessary and proper obligation of the state.

2. That many of the needy aged should be provided for outside of institutions where they may continue to live among friends and enjoy a sense of freedom, self-respect, and security.

The needy aged require shelter, food, clothing, and medical service. These are the first necessities. But no humane society can stop here: we must endeavor to furnish as well some of the things that make living worth while. No single program can bring this about immediately. The problem is, moreover, extremely complicated by the differences in human nature. Among the aged, many are sick. Many of these, but not all, need medical or institutional care. Some are mentally diseased, and, for their own sakes as well as for the protection of society, must be kept in hospitals and asylums. Some are able with a little systematic money help to balance their budgets and continue normal life, while others are too feeble or irresponsible to receive other than food, fuel, and clothing.

The existence of a group of needy aged, however, is recognized, who have maintained themselves usually throughout a lifetime by their own work and savings, and who have come to poverty in old age through no fault of their own. What they most want is to live out their lives among the old associations, with friends, neighbors, and the family, with appropriate work to do, and a sense of freedom, self-respect, and security. No progress can be made in this direction under the traditional administration of the old poor law and the almshouse—a tradition of stigma which it is believed will gradually disappear under the enlightened provisions of the new Public Welfare Act, a tradition which will be entirely obliterated so far as the aged are concerned by the enactment and efficient administration of the recommended act to provide old age security.

3. Responsibility for the administration of the recommended old

age security act should be placed jointly upon the county or city and the state.

After much deliberation, the commission rejected both exclusive state administration and exclusive local administration as a means for carrying out its program and recommended joint state and local administrative responsibilities.

Exclusive state administration was urged in order to bring about an immediate break with the old traditions of the poor law and the almshouse, to guarantee uniformity of administration throughout the state, and to relieve the localities of the tax burden of providing for the aged. These ends are desirable and are provided for under the plan recommended without the undesirable features of exclusive state management.

A state system would require a large department with scores of investigators traveling all over the state, visiting many of the same families cared for by local welfare officials, and supervising weekly grants for food, fuel, and rent where money allowances cannot be given wisely. It is not necessary to emphasize the duplication, the delay, the cost, and the bureaucracy that such a plan would require.

The Commission opposed exclusive county administration, though this is the plan which has been followed in all the American old age assistance systems, with the single exception of California, which has weak state supervision over the counties. Under exclusive county management there is danger that the law may be entirely ignored, or that it may be interpreted in the illiberal spirit of the old poor law, especially if the entire cost were to be placed upon the local taxpayers. If, however, the state shares part of the cost, the county allowances may be too generous, or in some cases influenced by political or other personal considerations.

As a protection against these dangers of county administration, the Commission recommended extensive supervision by the state. This supervision is provided through the powers of the state department of social welfare to prepare all forms and regulations; to suggest costs of living budgets for gauging assistance to the aged in various sections of the state; to examine and approve all reports of individual investigations; to make its own investigations where it suspects either insufficient or excessive allowances; to investigate and decide appeals from decisions of local welfare officials on request of the aged or their friends; to approve each grant in so far as it comes under the act, and finally to pass on the counties' claim for reimbursement by the state to the extent of 50 per cent on account of allowances paid and administrative expenses incurred. For the discharge of these functions, the Commission recommended the creation of a new division of old age security in the State Department of Social Welfare, believing that the State Department of Social Welfare, with these powers and an adequate appropriation, can produce uniformities throughout the state in the enforcement of the proposed old age security act, can bring about a marked departure from the undesirable features of the old poor law, and can protect the taxpayers of the state against unwarranted allowances.

With these protections there are many advantages in the proposed joint state and county or city system, because it will build upon the existing machinery of the new public welfare law, will hasten the gradual development of a strong unified local program of social welfare, and will eliminate duplication and confusion of agencies, offices, and investigations in each locality.

4. The financial responsibility for old age assistance should be divided equally between the state and the county or city welfare districts.

Two advantages seem apparent as a result of the adoption of this principle. Expenditures by the county or city are, in theory at least, closely scrutinized by the taxpayer. This is, in effect, a check to prodigality in the administration of the law and an assurance that the monies expended will be used for the purposes intended and for no other purpose. On the other hand, when the state itself has supervisory control, it will make for uniformity of administration, and further, with the state obligated for half the cost, it will tend to liberalize the viewpoint of county administrators. The Commission believes that joint financial responsibility is a corollary of joint administrative powers.

The three bills recommended by the commission were, first, An Act To Amend the Public Welfare Law, in relation to providing security against old age want; second, An Act Establishing a Division of Old Age Security in the Department of Social Welfare; and, third, An Act Giving Additional Power to the State Department of Social Welfare over existing county homes. It will be unnecessary to discuss the two latter acts or bills, as the first is the one of particular interest.[1]

This proposed act declares as its object that the care and relief of aged persons who are in need and whose physical or other conditions or disabilities render permanent their inability to provide properly for themselves is a special matter of state concern and a necessity in promoting the public health and welfare and establishes a state-wide system of old age relief at public expense for aged persons not in need of institutional care, such system to operate with such uniformity as the varying living conditions and costs of living permit. The term "relief" is defined to include assistance, aid, care, or support.

Old age relief is to be given to any person who

1. Has attained the age of seventy years.
2. Is unable to support himself, either in whole or in part; and has no children or other person able to support him and responsible under the provisions of the Public Welfare Act for his support.
3. Is a citizen of the United States.
4. Has been a resident of the state of New York for at least ten years immediately preceding his application for old age relief.
5. Resides in the public welfare district in which the application is made for at least one year immediately preceding the date of application.
6. Is not at the time an inmate of any public or private home for the aged, or any public home, or any public or private institution of a custodial, correctional, or curative character, except in the case of temporary medical or surgical care in a hospital.
7. Has not made a voluntary assignment or transfer of property for the purpose of qualifying for such relief.
8. Is not because of his physical or mental condition in need of continued institutional care.

It will be noted that there is no means qualification and no moral qualification. The means qualification was omitted, first, because it was not believed that it would be constitutional to define a poor person by reference to any means he might possess, and, second, be-

[1] Since the reading of this paper the first two of the bills have been unanimously passed by both houses of the Legislature and approved by the Governor, and are now known as Chapters 387 and 388 of the Laws of 1930, respectively. The third bill was not passed.

cause it was realized that in many cases the ownership of unproductive property would not be a test of need.

The old age relief to be given is defined as that which would provide adequately for those eligible, the amount and nature of the relief being fixed with due regard to the conditions existing in each case. No limitation in amount is made, the check on excessive allowance being in the supervision and approval or veto power residing in the State Department of Social Welfare. Old age relief may include, among other things, medical and surgical care and nursing. Otherwise relief may be granted only when it is practicable to care for an aged person in his own or some other suitable family home.

The application for relief may be made in person or by another in his behalf and shall be made to the public welfare official of the welfare district in which the applicant resides. An inmate of any public or private home for the aged, or of any public home, or of any public or private institution of a correctional, custodial, or curative character may make an application while in such home or institution, but the relief, if granted, shall not begin until after he ceases to be such inmate.

The public welfare district is to provide old age relief in the first instance subject to partial reimbursement by the state, and no part of the amounts expended by a county public welfare district shall be charged back to the town or city of the person's settlement within such county public welfare district.

The money for relief shall be annually appropriated by the legislative body of the public welfare district and be included in the taxes to be levied on the taxable property of the district. Provision is made for the raising of additional sums should the sum appropriated be expended or exhausted during the year and for the purpose for which it was appropriated.

The state is to reimburse each public welfare district to the extent of one-half of the amount expended for each aged person and shall also reimburse the public welfare district for one-half of the expenses of administering old age relief.

The claims for state reimbursement shall be presented by the respective welfare districts to the state department of social welfare semiannually in January and July.

Whenever a public welfare official receives an application for relief, an investigation and record shall be promptly made of the circumstances of the applicant. The object of such investigation shall be to ascertain the facts supporting the application and such other information as may be required by the rules of the state department of social welfare.

Upon the completion of such investigation the public welfare official shall decide whether the applicant is eligible for old age relief and the amount and nature of relief, if any, to be given. Each award made by the public welfare official shall be referred to the state department, and if approved by such department the decision shall be final. The public welfare official shall at the same time notify the applicant of the decision in writing. Provided, however, that in case any such application is not acted upon within thirty days after the filing of the application or is denied, or the award is deemed inadequate by the applicant, the applicant or someone in his behalf may appeal to the state department which upon receipt of such appeal may review the case. The state department may also, upon its own motion, review any decision made or any case in which a decision has not been made within the time specified. The state department may make such additional investigations as it may deem necessary and as the result of such investigation shall make such decision as to the granting of relief and the amount and nature of relief to be granted the applicant as in its opinion is just, and such decision shall be binding upon, and shall be complied with by, the public welfare official and the public welfare district involved.

Provision is also made for revocation of awards improperly granted or administered, and that periodic reconsideration of old age relief shall be had as frequently as may be required by the rules of the state department of social welfare. It is provided that it shall be within the power of the public welfare official at any time to cancel or revoke relief for cause or suspend payment of relief for such periods as he may deem proper, subject to the approval of the state department of social welfare.

It is required that each public welfare official report to the State Department of Social Welfare at such times and in such manner and form as the department may prescribe, the number of applications granted and the grants of relief changed, revoked, or suspended, together with copies of all applications and supporting affidavits.

The State Department of Social Welfare shall supervise the administration of old age relief by the public welfare officials and shall supply to them blanks for applications, reports, affidavits, and such other forms as it may deem advisable, having the power to make rules and regulations necessary for the carrying out of the provisions of the article to the end that old age relief may be administered uniformly throughout the state, having regard for the varying costs of living in different parts of the state and the compliance with the spirit and purpose of the act.

All relief given under the act shall be inalienable by any assignment or transfer and shall be exempt from levy or execution.

Penalties are provided for false statement or representation or by impersonation of an applicant or other fraudulent device to obtain old age relief for one who is not entitled thereto.

It is provided that the act shall take effect May 1, 1930, but that applications for relief shall not be made before September 1, 1930, and that relief shall not be granted to begin before January 1, 1931.

Upon the whole, the recommendations of the Commission have been received with expressions of genuine approval by the press and the citizens of the state of New York. Many have hailed it as the most progressive piece of social legislation proposed in the state during the last decade. On the other hand, it has been criticized from several different angles. The chief criticisms have been that it does not provide a maximum of money aid and that the administration is in substantially the same hands as was the administration of the old poor law and is now the administration of the public welfare act. As to the first criticism the commission was in grave doubts as to which course to pursue, whether to nominate a minimum sum which the state would assume or to place no limitation on the amount of aid. After much deliberation they took the latter view because of the wide differences in costs of living between the rural and urban, particularly New York City, districts of the state and because the medical, surgical, and nursing care the aged might require in the home would quickly use up any reasonable amount of aid or assistance.

It was thought best to leave it to the discretion of the public welfare officer with the approval of the State Department of Social Welfare as to how much should be allowed for the care and the need of each individual case.

With regard to the second objection, I have gone into the Commission's reasoning earlier in my discussion. We could not see the usefulness of setting up a new and distinct local agency to do the same work which the county welfare commissioner was already doing for those under the age of seventy. We felt that with the safeguards and appeals which we had thrown around the application and grant, the applicant would feel no sense of loss of self-respect in either making application for or receiving the grant. Another objection was that the age limit of seventy was too high and that sixty-five or even a lower age limit would be preferable. Any fixed limitation would, of course, result in hardships to some, but we felt that in the absence of definite data as to the numbers who would need old age assistance and of the consequent costs to the state, it was better to place the age at seventy, at which there could be no reasonable question, and find out from actual experience what the economic conditions were at that age.

Some criticisms have been made because the Commission did not recommend a contributory form of security, but the criticisms upon this point have been vague and indefinite in that they did not state whether the contributory form should be of a compulsory or a voluntary nature. The Commission considered both forms of contributions and learned that the voluntary contributory system had been a substantial failure wherever it was tried. The compulsory contributory system now in vogue in a number of European countries did not seem to the Commission to be adapted to the present industrial and economic condition of our state. It is undoubtedly true that a further study could be made along these lines which would be helpful and suggestive, but the Commission thought that the important problem was the relief of those today in want or those who would shortly be in want and who under no system of contribution were or could be in position to make contributions.

As chairman of the Commission, I feel assured that if the provisions of the act are systematically and effectively carried out, the result will be of untold blessing to those of our fellow-citizens who have looked forward to old age in poverty with terror and apprehension. We have provided a means whereby every aged citizen in need must be provided for if he so requests. The initiation for relief must for the most part come from those in need of relief, although under the provisions of the proposed act the application may be made by others in his behalf.

Personally, I believe that the act recommended by the Commission is a very definite advance in social welfare, particularly in that it is a recognition of an obligation by the state to the aged. Charity forms no part or parcel of our recommendation. The new principle which we have enunciated for our state is that of social obligation.

WISCONSIN'S EXPERIENCE WITH THE OLD AGE PENSION LAW

BENJAMIN GLASSBERG

Executive Director, Federation of Jewish Charities, Milwaukee, Wisconsin

It is very gratifying indeed to hear New York state, through Senator Seabury C. Mastick, frankly acknowledging the obligation resting upon the state to care for the aged. I feel we have made a tremendous step forward when that principle has been established. The details of the New York Pension Bill are not for the moment very important. After all, they are really secondary at this stage of the movement.

It often is the practice for speakers to take issue with the chairman, especially when his introductions are a bit too laudatory. While I do not like to be guilty of such a practice, I do want to stop for a moment to explain that after having lived in Wisconsin for a few years I have learned that it is not really as progressive as Easterners are fond of believing. An Old Age Pension Law and some other progressive measures it may have adopted, but until very recently, before the passage of the Children's Code it was far behind many other states in the field of social welfare legislation. In the administration of its penal institutions it still is far from progressive. However, one should not criticize one's own state and so I shall desist.

The Old Age Pension Law of Wisconsin was adopted in 1925, thus making Wisconsin the third state in the union to adopt such a measure. With the exception of Montana I believe my state has had more experience in the actual administration of an Old Age Pension Law than any other state in the union. There are, thus far, approximately four hundred pensioners on the lists in the few counties of the state where the law is in operation. Until January 1, 1930, only five of the smaller counties had adopted the Act. As in so many other states, the law is not mandatory but optional with the counties. The legislature when it passed the law did no more than accept the spirit and then proceeded to forget all about the law by leaving its enactment to the counties. This is an unsatisfactory method because

95

it appears to give the state something for which there has been a great deal of sentiment but in substance it gives very little. It was not until the fall of 1929 that Milwaukee County, for example, the only populous county in the state, adopted the Act. An effort made in the previous year to secure the adoption of the Act failed because a two-thirds majority could not be mustered in the county board of supervisors. This failure resulted in an amendment to the state law being passed which enabled the counties to adopt the law by a simple majority vote.

The preamble to the Wisconsin Old Age Pension Act reads as follows:

For the more humane care of aged dependent persons a state system of old age assistance is hereby established. Such system of old age assistance shall be administered in each county by the County Judge under the supervision of the Board of Control.

The word "pension" in the original law was stricken out in 1929 and for it was substituted the word "assistance." This is somewhat unfortunate because it is important to keep before the public the pension idea. On the other hand, "assistance" is more in keeping with the spirit in which the law is being administered.

California is not the only state which divides the cost of administration of the law between the state and county. Although the county must make the original outlay for all pensions granted, the law provides that it is to be reimbursed to the extent of one-third of the amount expended. The approval of the State Board of Control is necessary for such reimbursements. Wisconsin's experience with the administration of the Mother's Pension Law, where counties also are to be reimbursed one-third of the amount expended, would appear to indicate that this promise is not always carried out, due to the failure of the legislature to provide a sum large enough to make this possible.

Applications for old age assistance in Milwaukee county are filed with a temporary organization under the direction of the manager of Milwaukee County institutions, set up on January 1, 1930, when the law went into effect. It is planned, during the course of the year, to amalgamate the old age pension division with the department of outdoor relief so as to bring the administration of the law directly under the supervision of the superintendent of a reorganized department of public welfare.

A number of field workers have been assigned to the old age pension division who make thorough investigations of the social and financial status of the prospective pensioner. They file a written report with the judge of the county court who makes the decision as to the amount of the monthly pension to be granted. The county judge, unlike California and contrary to the terms of the New York Bill, plays a very important part in the administration of the law in Wisconsin, for he alone can fix the amount subject to the limitation of the law, which states that no one shall receive more than a dollar a day. There is a further limitation in that the county board may reduce the amount or suspend the pension entirely. In order to protect the interests of the county, an assistant district attorney is present at every hearing and when necessary takes steps to enforce the provisions of the law which charge children with the duty of caring for their parents.

The question might be raised as to the desirability of placing the power of granting a pension in the hands of the county judge, elected for various reasons, but among them certainly not on the ground of his understanding of the needs of the aged. It would appear to be much more desirable to place this responsibility in the hands of a board of public welfare chosen specifically for this and similar responsibilities.

As is the case in many other states which have adopted old age pension laws, the applicant must be seventy years of age to be eligible. In addition, he must have been a citizen of the United States for at least fifteen years before making application and he must have resided in the state and county in which he makes application for at least fifteen years. These provisions appear to me to be altogether too stringent. No doubt the residence requirement will be shortened in time, if we can go by the experience of the states with mother's pension laws. So long as only a few states have an old age pension system, there will be a fear that citizens from nearby states will rush to the state which grants pensions. In time, however, state legislatures will realize that people do not necessarily move from state to state because of the existence of a public pension plan. No doubt the small number of people who have thus far been granted pensions in Milwaukee County, with a population of over 600,000, is due largely to these provisions.

Unlike New York, there is a property qualification in the law. The Wisconsin law provides that an applicant who possesses property, the value of which is in excess of $3,000, is ineligible. An applicant may be required, as a condition to the grant of a pension, to transfer all or part of his property to the State Board of Control to be managed by it for his benefit. In the case of an applicant with property which is not used for the purpose of producing a reasonable income, the law provides that the annual income of such property shall be computed at 5 per cent of its value. The law further provides that on the death of a pensioner the total amount paid by the county with interest at 3 per cent shall be allowed and deducted from his estate, so that the county may be reimbursed wherever that is possible.

Payments are made by check, either monthly or quarterly. However, pensions may be revoked at any time if the county judge believes that conditions have changed to warrant such action. Funeral expenses are allowed up to one hundred dollars on the death of a pensioner. No other public assistance may be given a pensioner with the exception of medical and surgical help.

The New York Bill as outlined by Senator Mastick wisely avoids going into the morals of an applicant. The Wisconsin Bill, however, provides that no pension can be granted an applicant who, during the period of ten years immediately preceding his application has been imprisoned for a felony. In other words, a man's reputation must be beyond reproach if he is to enter the charmed circle of state pensioners, neither must he have been a habitual tramp or beggar during the year preceding his application.

Inmates of private or public homes for the aged are ineligible, although it will be recalled that California provides that inmates only of public homes for the aged are not eligible for assistance.

In the discussion of the California law at the conference, the question arose as to the wisdom of impressing upon applicants for old age pensions that they are actually receiving poor relief. Let me say that the same attitude prevails in the administration of the law in

Milwaukee. The fact that it has been placed under the supervision of the manager of the county institutions indicates pretty clearly that the law is regarded merely as another form of outdoor relief, and may I say in passing that I do not see how else the law can be administered until we provide for some form of old age insurance.

On January 1, 1930, the Old Age Assistance Law went into effect in Milwaukee County. During the first week or two, several hundred applications were made. During the past few weeks, however, there has been an average of about two or three a day applying. The total number of applicants for the first two months since the law went into effect is 572. Sixty per cent of the applicants are men. The number of cases actually disposed of is 183, and 95 of these have been granted pensions, not a very staggering amount to be sure. I do not believe that this number in any way indicates the extent to which the law will function in time. Although the newspapers have given a fair amount of publicity to the law, it has not always been of a favorable nature. The leading daily in the county has tended to emphasize the large amount spent in administration as against the small number of pensions granted.

Of the 88 cases which were disposed of unfavorably, only 14 applications were actually denied. Twenty-four were withdrawn, 47 were found not eligible and 3 died after making application. Of the 47 who were declared ineligible, 15 were denied a pension because they lacked the necessary citizenship requirement, 14, because they lacked the residence requirement, 8, because they possessed property or savings in excess of the amount allowed by the law, 9, because they were found to have earnings or a pension from other sources deemed sufficient for their support, and 1, because the children were able to support the applicant. There are still on file 395 applications out of the total of 572.

It is interesting to compare the amounts allotted to pensioners in Milwaukee with the five counties in the state which have adopted the law, as is shown in Table I.

It should be noted that whereas 83 per cent of the pensioners in Milwaukee County were granted $20 a month or more, only 43 per cent or half as many received such pensions in the five counties of the state.

The total amount spent by the state of Wisconsin until January 1, 1929, after the law had been in effect four years, was $170,000. The average monthly pension is $20 per capita.

Just a few facts about those on the pension list in the state, exclusive of Milwaukee, for whom no detailed information is as yet available. We find that 46 per cent of those receiving pensions in the state are physically disabled. Only 15 out of the 290 receiving pensions report any earnings. Thirty-four per cent have no other source of income. This is interesting in view of the fact that according to the report of the State Board of Control only 11 per cent were grant-

TABLE I

AMOUNT OF MONTHLY PENSION	MILWAUKEE COUNTY*		IN COUNTIES OTHER THAN MILWAUKEE†	
	Number of Pensioners	Per Cent of Total	Number of Pensioners	Per Cent
$30.00	20	21	32	11
25–29	34	36	27	9
20–24	25	26	68	23.5
15–19	11	11.5	121	41.7
5–14	5	5.5	42	14.8
Total	95	100	290	100

* For period January–February, 1930.
† For year ending December 31, 1928.

ed the maximum allowance of $30 a month. Evidently the percentage should have been much higher in view of the fact that three times as many as were granted $30 a month had no other source of income.

Almost half of the pensioners we find were in domestic service, 80 of the 290 having been housewives. Apparently this is an occupation to be avoided. Only three of the pensioners were engaged in clerical work. They seemed to reach old age in somewhat better shape than the stalwart followers of manufacturing and agriculture. In rural districts where one would expect that most people would own their homes and farms, we find that 72 per cent of the pensioners do not own their homes or any land. Only 7 per cent were found to have any savings. The possibility of support from children has been stressed in the course of the conference. The State Board of

Control on an examination of the financial condition of the children of those in receipt of pensions states that "they are not making any more than a living for themselves and their family." This is a rather striking statement in view of the fact that 33 per cent of those receiving pensions are also receiving some help from their children. Now either one statement or the other is incorrect. It is peculiar to find that although in none of the cases are the children doing more than making a living for themselves, nevertheless a good many are actually giving assistance to parents in receipt of a pension, undoubtedly at the expense of the health or education of the grandchildren.

It seems to me that the New York Bill ought to be commended for not making any definite provision as to the amount of pension to be granted, as is the case in all other states. In the final analysis, the pension granted is based upon some investigation as to the financial status of the applicant. Including a definite maximum in the law often makes it impossible, especially if the amount is a dollar a day, to grant a sum sufficiently large to enable an aged person to supply all of his wants. Any sum is bound in time to become a hindrance since the value of the dollar fluctuates. Last year the Children's Code Bill of Wisconsin provided for a revision of the Mother's Pension Law, and it omitted completely any specific monthly allowances. Instead the law provides for a budget system. The court is to determine the amount needed to maintain a given family. It takes into consideration whatever resources the family has and the amount of the state aid is to represent the difference between its needs and its income. If this is what the New York Bill contemplates, then I say it is moving in the right direction so long as we do not have a contributory pension system.

In those states where the legislature is not yet ready to take such a step, it seems to me that there ought to be an increase in the maximum amount to be granted to applicants for old age pensions.

An objection to the Old Age Pension Law has often been raised on the ground that it gives no consideration to the man who has managed to save something toward his old age. It is claimed that Jones who reaches seventy with no savings is to receive a dollar a day, whereas Smith who has an income of let us say $50 or $75 a year from his savings and who perhaps has been accustomed to living on a slightly higher standard than Jones, does not get any consideration under the law and will receive a smaller pension than Jones. Without attempting to enter into the field of morals or ethics, it seems to me that a recent bill introduced in Congress for the District of Columbia serves to answer this criticism in that it excludes from the determination of an applicant's income an amount up to $100 which may be derived from savings or lodge or union pension so that such an applicant would have this sum in addition to the state pension, and thereby enable him to benefit from his savings and also to maintain that slightly higher standard to which he is accustomed.

PENSIONS AS A PART OF A SOCIAL
INSURANCE PROGRAM

JOHN A. LAPP

Marquette University, Milwaukee, Wisconsin

I should like to speak informally tonight. In view of the fact that I have not been present at the other sessions I may touch upon subjects that have been discussed heretofore in this Conference. But, at any rate, I want to go over certain ground, and I am going to be somewhat dogmatic in my statements. I believe what I believe on the subject of social insurance and am so thoroughly convinced of some of the things that I believe that I have no hesitation in speaking dogmatically on them. And, therefore, if I appear to be dogmatic in this proceeding tonight, you will understand that my faith is firmly set, particularly on the subject of old age pensions. There are some things that I want to state. In the first place, people do get old. No one will deny that. I think it should be understood, too, that more people get old than ever before; that there are more old people than ever before in proportion to the total population. In fact, there are 500,000 more people over sixty-five today than the normal number, on account of the great improvement in health and longevity. We have what we would have had under the condition of twenty years ago plus 500,000 people over sixty-five at this time. It is perfectly obvious, too, that the opportunities for work for people over fifty-five or sixty have lessened. I will state another thing with a good deal of dogmatism, namely: that as things stand to-day, we cannot rely upon thrift to provide for old age. We cannot rely upon the savings of people at sixty-five to support them for the rest of their life in even a minimum amount of decency or comfort. Having stated these things, the proposition that naturally follows is that there must be certain provisions at sixty or sixty-five years of age to care for people who have been unable to provide for the means of living beyond that time.

It is quite probable that if we had a scheme of social insurance, thoroughly organized, covering sickness, unemployment, and accidents and some kind of social insurance against business failures, and if we had greater assurance that men would have a living wage throughout their careers, and if we made sure that people were going to be trained vocationally and otherwise to fit them for the occupations of life, and if some other things were provided socially that I haven't time to mention, we could assume that a larger percentage of people would approach sixty-five years of age with some means of a livelihood thereafter.

But even with the best of social protections that we can give, we cannot hope that any very large percentage of our people at sixty-five years of age will be self-supporting for that uncertain length of years—perhaps one year, perhaps thirty—beyond the time when they cease to work. A complete plan of social insurance is an expectation that cannot soon be fulfilled. We will go on expanding our workmen's compensation laws. We have had very good results thus far in expanding them. Many remember the first compensation laws that were passed. Those who are pessimistic about the crudity of the old age pension laws and their inadequacy might reflect upon the inadequacies of the workmen's compensation laws when they were first passed. Provisions were made for a mere fraction of the wages, medical care up to $50, medical care in some states for the first week or two weeks only; compensation stopped right at the point when it was needed most. It is most interesting to go through the first laws enacted back in 1912 and 1913 in the majority of the states and observe how inadequate they were. We will go on expanding the laws and take care of a larger and larger portion of the loss to workmen from the cause of accidents; at present the workers bear fully 65 per cent of the losses.

In due time, we will have a broad and inclusive system of health insurance. For one, I have kept faith, in the midst of the vicissitudes of the campaign. It is fixed in the stars that we are going to have health insurance in due time in some form or other and quite completely. It may not come to gladden the heart of Dr. Rubinow, the real founder of the movement in this country, or myself, or any of the pioneers in the movements, but it will come.

I do not see any very great prospect of adequate protection against business failures. And yet such failures are the source of much of our poverty. We have had 8,000 bank failures in the United States since 1920. About 25 per cent in number of all the banks in the United States have failed since 1920. The figures of casualties among business enterprises run to colossal size, and the number of people, that have been driven into poverty by virtue of this, is, of course, almost incalculable. From the point of view of old age protection it is worth while to recall what happened to the New Englanders in the case of the New York, New Haven, and Hartford Railrod. For years the bonds and stocks of that company were a favorite investment. Everybody that had trust funds put them into these safe stocks and bonds. People put their trust in them for old age. All through New England and New York were found thousands who were dependent upon the New York, New Haven, and Hartford Railroad for their care in old age. But the railroad failed, and only a small percentage of the securities were redeemed. I think it would be worth making a survey in this case to see the extent to which old age dependency has resulted to people who otherwise would have had adequate protection.

When it comes to the failure of corporations, I have little to suggest as a solution. We are a country of calamity when it comes to business failures. We have some protection against natural calamities. We are already developing social insurance against such calamities as hail. Farmers who might lose their crops, and perhaps their farms, are being protected in the Dakotas by state-wide systems of hail insurance. When greater protections are secured against the calamities of life we can approach the subject of old age pensions with greater assurance that we will not have quite the burden that we now may expect.

Coming now to old age security, I have certain dogmatic ideas with respect to what we should do. I am a confirmed believer in the system of state or public pensions. I have no expectation, no confidence, in any plan of old age insurance carried out in the United States of America. Those of my confrères here who have agreed with me on many other questions may find disagreement here. But upon considerable study I do not deem it possible to establish in the United States or in any state a system of contributory old age insurance that would be adequate and that administratively would be within the range of reasonable expectation. Any system that collects premiums from workers from the time that they start to work until they are sixty-five involves expenses that would take at the very least a third to a half of the fund for administration. When we contemplate the difficulty growing out of shifting employments and shifting of men from city to city and state to state, when you look at some of the metropolitan communities like New Jersey and New York and realize how state lines have been wiped out, I think it will appear that insurance by states at least is out of the question.

I have no expectation either, and I think most of us have little, that the pension systems of private industry will ever solve but a tiny fraction of the problem. At best, there is only a small portion of the employees who can expect to have lifelong work with one industry. Moreover, the employees of small concerns could not be thus protected. I know of no insurance in this country, outside of some of the police department pensions, where the widows are taken care of by any form of service pensions. Yet considerably more than half of the aged population is composed of women, widows who could not come under a pension system of the service character. Of course, we might conceive the idea that when the men are insured the insurance of the wife be included. I doubt, however, if that will ever be adopted widely; the expense would be more than doubled and that would be a powerful deterrent. Women have a longer expectation of life after sixty-five years. The only way to care for widows without adequate means of support will be by public pensions out of the public treasury.

Another consideration usually overlooked is the probable status of single women employees as they grow old. We know that women's employments at present are such that they require young women. What does the future hold for the factory girl at fifty? Or even the clerk or business woman? We may guess that their chances in old age are not likely to be as good even as those of the men.

The second dogmatic statement that I would like to express (perhaps it is the third or fifth or tenth) is that the age of seventy is absurd—quite absurd under present conditions. We are giving no attention in the new pension laws to what happens to people from the time they are no longer able to work until the seventieth birthday. If the statements are true that people cannot find work after fifty-five or are thrown out of work at fifty-five or at most at sixty, ten years intervene. There is ample time to suffer, ample time to starve, between the time of the loss of work until the seventieth year.

Another thing I want to emphasize out of the discussion this afternoon. I sympathize most heartily with the idea that we must keep this system just as free as possible from connection with outdoor relief. I am as convinced of that subject as I am of any subject under the sun, and I regret very much to see the tendency to put the administration of old age pensions into the hands of the same officials who are administering outdoor relief. For we ought to conceive of old age pensions as being for the benefit of another group of people in between those whom we designate as paupers and those who are fortunate enough to save sufficient to protect themselves. We should reach that group in a way that would not be denominated charity by them and would not be so understood by the general public. I would like to see the term "pension" even though it isn't according to Webster, used, emphasized, kept to the front, and never lost sight of in connection with the old age pensions that we are planning for. What does it matter if the word is not just exactly correctly used by those who understand that it is something different from outdoor relief.

There are some devices that I think old age pension systems ought to adopt, and I am sorry that the laws have not thus far put them into effect. It seems as though there could be a combination for the promotion of thrift along with the granting of pensions that would provide all that the individual seeks. Suppose we adopt the age of sixty-five years as the age when pensions shall begin. Let us assume that at sixty-five years a person qualifies for a pension at a dollar a day, and having qualified, if he chooses to remain off the pension fund for a year or two years or three years, if he can eke out an existence some way, the pension will accumulate for him an additional annuity. So if he stays off an extra year or two he may receive a dollar and a quarter a day. If he can get along somehow for five years after qualifying, the pension might be double the original pension. This plan would encourage people to use every possible effort to take care of themselves and would encourage relatives to help, because as they grow older, the aged person would have a more and more adequate pension to take care of him.

The second proposal would be for some sort of a public insurance or annuity scheme managed by the public authorities for insurance in addition to the pension. Let us make it possible for individuals and for groups, labor unions, mutual benefit societies, employees' groups, teachers, policemen, etc., to insure in a state fund for the additional payment of annuities. Such insurance should of course follow the worker regardless of whether he stays in the employment of a certain company or not. A device should be worked out also for those who can exercise additional thrift thus providing larger funds for old age support than we now have.

Going back just a bit, I want to refer to another subject discussed previously in this Conference, namely, the question of holding relatives responsible for support. In other words, if children are found, able to support the parents, the pension should not be granted. I would express my strong condemnation of an attempt by an uncertain standard to measure the ability of children to care for their aged parents. We should insist of course, that those who are amply able should contribute to the support of their aged parents. But I would not favor the idea of imposing upon a man and a wife and family the necessity of contributing a penny toward the support of an aged parent when the wage is not sufficient to take care of the family itself, unless in fact there is an adequate margin for the purpose above the living wage.

For there is a legal principle involved in such cases. We have a third party in this combination. We have not merely the child of the aged person, we have a wife or husband also. We have a third party, who has no personal obligation to support the parent of wife or husband. We cannot impose rightly upon the young family obligations that are beyond their reasonable ability to carry.

Moreover, it is hard to conceive of any outdoor relief agencies or any social workers capable of determining what in each case should be the limit of people's ability to pay. There are very few, indeed, of the people affected by old age pension whose children are able to contribute anything, as was said this afternoon, to the support of their parents without depriving their own children of that which rightly belongs to them.

Well, much that I have gone over is old ground. I have not expressed, I know, anything particularly new, even though I may have said some things with a considerable degree of positiveness. I expect to see old age pension systems advance. I expect to see old age pension laws enacted pretty generally throughout the country within another five or ten years. I expect to see additions to the groundwork that has been laid as in the case of the workmen's compensation laws; I anticipate that old age pensions will be quite adequately provided throughout the nation. I wish it were possible —it is possible constitutionally—to secure a system of grants in aid of old age pensions from the Federal Treasury. The Federal government is better able to provide the necessary funds than any community. It can equalize the burden over the whole country, and there is not a more powerful instrument for the promotion of things for the common good than the system of grants in aid. We use this system in granting aid from the states to the counties for old age pensions already, and the plan is in operation in the Dominion of Canada.

So while I have added little that is new, I have expressed my faith in the scheme of social insurance. Health insurance has lagged for the time being; workmen's compensation has gone on apace; old age pensions are moving ahead; other forms of social protection are in the beginning. We may compare the present position to that of the line of an advancing army. The right wing, workmen's compensation, has pushed far out into the enemy's lines. The center, health insurance, has been pressed back behind its original position. The left wing, old age pensions, is on the move and is gradually driving farther and farther into the enemy's territory. With the two wings going forward, it is only a matter of time when the line will be straightened and new offensives will be planned for the realization of the goal of social protection.

APPENDIX A
NOTE ON THE CARE OF THE AGED IN ILLINOIS

[EDITORIAL NOTE.—The following brief statement concerning the care of the aged in the state of Illinois was prepared in advance of the conference and was distributed to the members in mimeographed form to facilitate discussion of the Illinois problem. Since the reader may also be glad to have these facts in hand, they are presented here.]

The number of persons aged sixty-five years and over who are now being assisted in Illinois by public or private agencies of one sort or another cannot be accurately determined. Certain data are, however, available as a result of a series of recent publications,[1] and these data have been assembled for the convenience of the Conference.

TABLE I

AGE OF ILLINOIS ALMSHOUSE POPULATION
ENUMERATED AS OF JANUARY 1, 1923

Age	Number	Per Cent Distribution
All ages..................	6,415	100.0
Under sixty-five years of age..	3,169	49.4
Sixty-five years or over......	3,209	50.0
Age not reported............	37	0.6

One hundred almshouses were listed in Illinois at the time of the census of "Paupers in Almshouses" in 1910, and these almshouses had a total population of 5,421. The Cook County Infirmary at Oak Forest had 1,859 inmates in 1910, and the next largest almshouse in the state was the LaSalle County Asylum with 187.

A recent census of Oak Forest, which was made in connection with a study that was carried on by the Graduate School of Social Service, showed that half of all the inmates were sixty-five years of age and over. Table II is a result of that census.

[1] United States Bureau of the Census, *Paupers in Almshouses, 1923* (Washington, D.C.: Government Printing Office, 1925); United States Bureau of Labor Statistics, Bulletin No. 386 (1925), *The Cost of American Almshouses*, by Estelle M. Stewart; *idem*, Bulletin No. 489 (1929), *Care of Aged Persons in the United States*, by Florence E. Parker, Estelle M. Stewart, and Mary Conymgton; *idem*, Bulletin No. 505 (1929), *Directory of Homes for the Aged in the United States;* Chicago Pension Commission, *Report of the Pension Commission of the City of Chicago, submitted August 31, 1927* (Chicago, 1927); Chicago Department of Public Welfare, *Care of the Aged in Chicago*, by Elizabeth A. Hughes and Elsie M. Wolcott (Chicago, 1927).

A study of the "Cost of American Almshouses" made November, 1923, to November, 1924, by the United States Bureau of Labor Statistics contains the following information about the 90 Illinois institutions which reported. The value of the property of these 90 almshouses, including land, farm equipment,

TABLE II

AGE OF OAK FOREST POPULATION ENUMERATED AS OF DECEMBER 1, 1928

AGE	BOTH SEXES		MEN		WOMEN	
	Number	Per Cent Distribution	Number	Per Cent Distribution	Number	Per Cent Distribution
All ages...............	3,500	100.0	2,762	100.0	738	100.0
Under sixty-five years of age	1,733	49.5	1,374	49.7	359	48.6
Sixty-five or over.........	1,754	50.1	1,382	50.1	372	50.4
Age not reported.........	13	0.4	6	0.2	7	1.0

buildings, and furnishings was $14,633,819. The value per inmate was $2,577.29. The net annual income of these institutions from public funds, sale of farm produce, and all other sources was $1,857,465; the annual maintenance cost $1,831,104; the maintenance cost per inmate, $322.49. These institutions varied in size and cost of maintenance per inmate as shown in Table III.

TABLE III

Number of Institutions of Specified Size	Total Inmates	Maintenance Cost	Value of Land, Farm Equipment, Buildings, and Furnishings per Inmate	Cost of Maintenance per Inmate
16 (1–10 inmates)..........	81	$ 35,224	$1,595.68	$434.86
31 (11–25 inmates).........	528	174,808	1,480.77	331.07
23 (26–50 inmates).........	804	298,922	1,626.51	371.79
13 (51–100 inmates)........	853	248,664	1,743.29	291.52
6 (101–200 inmates).......	857	201,382	1,094.95	234.99
1 (over 2,000 inmates).....	2,555	872,105	2,739.73	341.33

CARE OF OLD PERSONS IN HOMES FOR THE AGED

The directory of homes for the aged in the United States issued by the U.S. Bureau of Labor Statistics in November, 1929, lists 78 private homes for the aged with a capacity varying from 9 to 250 and a combined accommodation of 5,133 in the 70 homes reporting. The admission age was as low as fifty or fifty-five for 2 homes, sixty for 14, sixty-two for 1, sixty-five for 37, sixty-eight for 1, and seventy for 5 homes. Entrance fees varied from $100 to $3,000 with the most common fee $500. Fifty-five homes accommodated both men and women, 2 accepted men only, and 15 took women only.

Forty-two of these homes situated in Chicago or its near vicinity have a capacity of about 3,600.

Over half these private homes for the aged are sponsored by religious groups, about 1 in 9 is conducted for and by a special nationality, and about 1 in 10 by a fraternal organization or a trade union. Being able to care for oneself is generally an admission requirement to any of these homes not definitely established to care for disabled or incurables.

In the United States as a whole, per capita cost in homes conducted by labor organizations averages $834.35 per annum; in those carried on by religious organizations, per capita expense varies from $83.33 to $1,631.83 and averages around $436.89 a year; homes operated by fraternal organizations vary from $33 to $911.00 and average $457.00; the homes for various nationality groups average $346.00 in per capita cost. The average cost in private benevolent homes in Illinois was $488.10; in the Old Peoples Home of Chicago, $529.01.

CARE OF THE AGED BY FEDERAL, STATE, OR LOCAL GOVERNMENT

The number of war pensioners in Illinois in 1927–28 was 33,096. The annual value of the pensions paid to them was $15,536,116.

A national Home for Disabled Volunteer Soldiers is located at Danville, Illinois, and the state of Illinois maintains the Illinois Soldiers' and Sailors' Home at Quincy (capacity 1,500) and the Soldiers' Widows' Home at Wilmington (capacity 115). The average number in residence at these state homes is 730 and the annual cost of operation $486.00 per capita.

Illinois has examples also of public employees' retirement pensions covering teachers, police, firemen, and certain other municipal, county, or state employees. In 1926, Illinois had 1,486 retired teachers on pensions which averaged $381.00 per annum; Chicago, 973 on an average pension of $665.00 a year.

In Chicago nine pension funds for public employees are in existence. In 1927, these funds covered 33,366 employees and had 7,243 beneficiaries with an average pension of $593.54.

Figures are not available for the number of aged receiving outdoor relief in the state. In Cook County, however, 1,100 persons at least sixty-five years old were assisted once or more in 1929.

CARE BY LABOR ORGANIZATIONS

Besides the care in homes for the aged already mentioned, at least ten trade unions have old age pension plans which affect the members of these unions resident in Illinois. In 1927, at least 561 pensioners of 8 union pension plans were living in Chicago. Pensions in 3 of these plans were $7.00 or $8.00 a week; in 4, $25.00 or $35.00 a month; and in 1 plan the minimum pension was $50.00 a month.

INDUSTRIAL PENSION PLANS

In 1927, 105 industrial pension plans were affecting the employees of as many industrial companies in Chicago. Thirty-seven of these plans had no pensioners in Chicago in that year, 9 of those with pensioners could not estimate at all how many retired employees they had on an allowance in the city, and 59 stated they were paying pensions to 3,300—3,400 former employees in this area. In two-thirds of these industrial pension plans, the minimum pension ranged from $60.00 to $364.00 per annum; 4 plans paid less than $1.50 a day, 3 paid $600.00, $650.00, or $900.00 a year, and 1 had a minimum pension of $1,200.00.

The pension plans of religious denominations should also be mentioned, whereby aged ministers and their widows or other dependents are cared for.

APPENDIX B
DIGEST OF STATE LAWS ON OLD AGE SECURITY
ALASKA

LAWS OF ALASKA, 1929, CHAP. 65

An act to revise and codify the laws relative to the care and support of the destitute or needy. Approved April 30, 1929, to take effect immediately.

Alaska Pioneers' Home.—To be maintained at Sitka for the "care of such needy persons as shall be entitled to the benefits thereof."

Administration: Board of Trustees, three in number; governor, to serve as chairman and member and appoint the other two, one of whom is to act as secretary and receive a salary of $75 a month, the other, as treasurer, at $50 a month.

Their powers and duties cover the care, control, and management of the Home, the disbursement of the funds appropriated for the operation of the institution, the making of contracts for furnishings and supplies, the appointment of the superintendent, and other officials, and the adoption of rules and regulations regarding the government, admission, and expulsion of inmates.

Requirements for admission: Every worthy person continuously resident in Alaska for more than 5 years immediately preceding application, who is destitute, and in need of the aid or benefit of the Home in consequence of physical disability or for other cause is eligible to admission for free care. A person whose support and maintenance is imposed by law upon a relative or member of his family is not to be admitted. A person who is insane is to be transferred to a sanitarium.

Admission on payment is possible for any United States citizen sixty-five years of age or over, continuously resident in the territory for not less than 10 years immediately preceding application, but not destitute, upon agreement to pay the territory such sum per day as the Board of Trustees deems sufficient to compensate for the cost of his care and support at the Home.

Maintenance: The legislature appropriates the necessary funds to be expended by the Board of Trustees.

Pensions.—The Board of Trustees may allow a pension to any resident of Alaska, a citizen of the United States, sixty-five years old or over if a man, sixty or more if a woman, who has resided continuously in Alaska since January 1, 1906, and is entitled to free benefits in the Alaska Pioneers' Home. The aged person must make application for an allowance, the Board then investigates, and "if it finds the case worthy and the person in actual need" of such an allowance, enrols him as a beneficiary under this Act, issues a non-transferable, non-descendable certificate, and the pension becomes payable out of the allowances to aged pioneers. Any inmate of the Home may at any time apply for such an allowance if eligible. If a person on the allowance goes into the Home, however, his allowance is suspended for the period of his residence there.

Application: The Board of Trustees is to issue blanks to the commissioners of the precincts to be filled out, signed, sworn to, and verified by the affidavit of two reputable persons resident in the precinct, under penalty of perjury for false statement, and to cover in detail such facts as periods and causes of any disability for gaining subsistence, the resources and circumstances of the applicant, and of his relatives, and to state that the applicant is dependent upon an allowance from the Territory and has no other means of support.

Amount of Allowance: Shall not exceed $35 a month for men and $45 a month for women. The Trustees are to fix the sum and state it in the certificate which they grant the aged person. The Board may at any time demand of the beneficiary a signed and sworn statement as to his disability for gaining a subsistence. The amount of the allowance is to be based upon need and not to be a uniform amount. It shall take into account the necessities of each individual and the cost of living in the community where he resides. The Board may alter the amount of the pension or discontinue it as it sees fit.

Payment is to be made quarterly by warrant of the Board of Trustees on the territorial treasurer through the commissioner in whose precinct the beneficiary resides.

Payments outside the territory are possible if the person granted the allowance wishes to reside elsewhere and the Board is willing to permit him to do so.

The Trustees may, if the beneficiary seems to them to be wasteful of the funds or to be using them for something besides subsistence, pay the allowances to a depositary for use for the beneficiary.

Medical Certificate: A medical certificate is required for admission to the Home. Any inmate of the Home eligible to an allowance must submit with his application a certificate from a practicing physician not connected with the Home setting forth the state of his health.

ARIZONA

Laws of Arizona, 1915, Initiative Measures, p. 10

An act providing for an old age and mothers' pension and making appropriation therefor. Approved November 3, 1914. In effect by proclamation of the governor, dated December 14, 1914.

All almshouses within the state shall be abolished, their grounds and buildings shall be sold for the best obtainable price, and the proceeds shall be devoted for the purpose hereafter set forth in this act.

In absence of almshouses, and in order to care for aged people and people incapable of earning a livelihood by reason of physical infirmities and widows or wives whose husbands are in penal institutions or insane asylums, they being mothers of children who are under the age of sixteen years, a system of pensioning is hereby established.

Administration.—The Arizona State Board of Control shall have entire charge of all funds provided for the purpose mentioned, and shall order the same paid by the state treasurer to persons entitled, upon warrant issued by the boards of supervisors of the various counties in the state of Arizona. These boards shall also act as examining boards on the fitness and eligibility of applicants for pensions.

Qualifications of claimants.—Sixty years of age and upward; citizens of the United States; residents of Arizona for 5 years last preceding application; without visible means of support.

Grant.—$15 a month as long as such pensioners shall continue to live within this state.

Source of funds.—There is hereby appropriated out of the general fund of the state treasury a sufficient amount each year to carry out and put into effect the provisions of this act.

[NOTE.—The foregoing measure was submitted to the people by initiative petition, filed July 2, 1914, and approved by a majority of the votes cast thereon at the general election held on the third of November, 1914. Before the act could become effective, however, it was pronounced unconstitutional on the ground of its vagueness and loose wording.]

CALIFORNIA

STATUTES AND AMENDMENTS TO THE CODES, 1929, CHAP. 530

An act to provide for the protection, welfare, and assistance of aged persons in need and resident in the state of California. Approved May 28, 1929. In effect August 14, 1929.

Construction.—Nothing in this act shall be construed as repealing any other act or part of an act providing for the support of the poor except in so far as inconsistent therewith, and the provisions of this act shall be construed as an additional method of support and provision for the aged poor. This act shall be liberally construed.

Administration.—The Division of State Aid to the Aged is created in the State Department of Social Welfare. This division is to be administered by a chief, "who shall be a person with training and experience in relief work and familiar with the social and economic conditions in California," appointed by the director of the department of social welfare with the approval of the governor and members of the Social Welfare Board of the department. The chief of the division shall be responsible for the investigation, determination, and supervision of state aid given under this act.

Duties of division: To supervise and pass upon the measures taken by county or city and county boards of supervisors for the care of the needy aged citizens, to the end that they may receive suitable care in their old age and that there may be throughout the state a uniform standard of record and method of treatment of aged persons based upon their individual needs and circumstances.

Policy: The state department through its division of state aid to the aged and each Board of Supervisors shall follow the policy of giving the aid provided under this act to each and every applicant in his own or some other suitable home in preference to placing him in an institution.

Local: In addition to their other powers and duties in the care and support of the poor, the boards of supervisors shall receive and act upon applications under this act, provide funds in their respective county or city and county treasury, and do all other acts and things necessary for the purpose of carrying out the provisions of this act in so far as they relate to a county or city and county.

Advisory boards: The chief of the division of state aid to the aged with the approval of the director of the department may appoint in each county or city and county an advisory board of citizens whose duty it shall be to co-operate with the proper state and county authorities in the investigation and supervision of aid to the aged and to make report with recommendations to the board of supervisors and to the department of social welfare. Existing county departments of public welfare or boards with similar functions in public relief shall be appointed as the advisory boards.

Powers of the department: The department shall have the power to prescribe the form of the application for aid, the manner and form of all reports, and to make any additional rules and regulations necessary for carrying out the provisions of this act.

Qualifications of claimants.—Subject to the provisions of this act, every person residing in California, if in need, shall be entitled to aid in old age from the state. Aid may be granted to any person who—

1. Has attained the age of seventy years.

2. Has been a citizen of the United States for at least 15 years before making application for aid.

3. Resides in California and has so resided continuously for at least 15 years immediately preceding the date of application or has so resided 40 years at least 5 of which have immediately preceded application.

4. Resides in the county or the city and county in which the application is made and has so resided for at least 1 year immediately preceding application.

5. Is not at application for aid an inmate of any prison, jail, infirmary, insane asylum, or any reform or correctional institution.

6. If married, has not during 15 years preceding application deserted his spouse or without just cause failed to provide legal support for spouse and minor children, if any.

7. Has no child or other person able to support him and responsible under the law of this state for his support.

Aid under this áct shall not be granted to or paid to any person the value of whose property exceeds $3,000 at time of application, or if married, if the combined property of husband and wife exceeds this amount.

Grant.—The amount of aid shall be fixed with due regard to the conditions existing in each case, but in no case shall it, when added to the income of the applicant from all other sources, income from property included, exceed a total of $1 a day.

Application: Every applicant shall file in writing an application with the board of supervisors of his county of residence in the manner and form prescribed by the state department. All statements in the application are to be verified under oath by the applicant. The board shall directly or through the advisory board or other agency make investigation promptly and decide the amount of aid to be granted if any, and such decision shall be final except that if the application is denied the case may be appealed to the department of social welfare.

All payments shall be made monthly by the treasurer of the county or city and county of residence. All aid shall be renewed annually on verified applications, and after such further investigations as the board may deem necessary. The amount of aid is subject to change with change in the applicant's circumstances. It is within the power of the board of supervisors to cancel or revoke aid for cause or to suspend payments for such periods as it deems necessary. It is the duty of a recipient to notify the board immediately of any change in the amount of the property or income. If through concealment or failure to notify the board of the amount of property or income, the aid given is larger than required, the department may recover from the estate as a preferred claim.

Transfer of property: The board of supervisors may with the consent of the department require as a condition to the grant or continuance of aid that all or part of property of the applicant be transferred to the board to be managed by it and the income to go to the person aided.

Aid inalienable: The aid is inalienable by any assignment, sale, attachment, execution, or otherwise.

Penalties and offenses.—If the state department at any time has reason to think aid has been improperly obtained, it shall cause special inquiry and may suspend payment of the allowance. If improperly granted it shall be cancelled. For obtaining aid fraudulently or aiding and abetting a person so to do, the penalty is that for a misdemeanor and is fixed at a fine of not over $500 or imprisonment for not over 6 months or both. The punishment for knowingly violating any provision of the act is similar.

Reports.—The clerk of the board of supervisors shall report monthly to the state department as the department prescribes. This report shall cover the number of applications granted, the grants of aid changed, revoked, or suspended by the board in the month, copies of all applications received and a statement of the action taken on each, and the amount of aid to aged paid out under this act. Claims for state aid granted shall be presented by the counties semi-annually. When the prescribed procedure has been completed, the state treasurer shall pay to the treasurer of the county or city and county a sum equal to one-half of the total amount of payments made by the county to aged citizens under this act for the period of the claim.

Source of funds.—All necessary expense incurred by the county or city and county boards of supervisors and advisory boards shall be paid by the county or city and county in the same manner as its other expenses.

There is appropriated out of the state treasury to each and every county or city and county maintaining and supporting aged persons within the provisions of this act, aid not in excess of $180 per annum for each aged person so aided by the county or city and county.

To the department of social welfare, $20,000 is appropriated for expenses in administering this act in the eighty-first and eighty-second fiscal years.

COLORADO

SESSION LAWS OF COLORADO, 1927, CHAP. 143

An act relating to old age pensions, and to provide for the assistance of aged indigent persons under certain conditions. Approved and in effect March 19, 1927.

By affirmative vote of two-thirds of the members elected to the Board of County Commissioners in any county, any county may establish a system of old age pensions. After at least 1 year under such a system, the county may abandon it.

Administration.—The Board of County Commissioners is to make rules and regulations and publish such information as it may deem advisable in order to acquaint aged persons and the public generally with this old age pension plan.

The county judge is to make an investigation to determine the qualifications of applicants, decide upon each application and fix the amount of the pension with the approval of the Board of County Commissioners within 30 days of the filing of the application, and this decision of judge and Board shall be final.

Qualifications of claimants.—Any person who complies with the provisions of this act while resident in a county or city and county which maintains a system of old age pensions is entitled to pension. The pension may be granted only to a person who—

1. Is seventy years of age or over.
2. Has been a citizen of the United States for at least 15 years preceding.
3. Has been continuously resident in the state and in the county or city and county in which he makes application for at least 15 years immediately preceding.
4. Is not an inmate of any prison, jail, workhouse, infirmary, insane asylum, or other public correctional institution.
5. Has not in the 10 years immediately preceding been imprisoned for felony.
6. Has not, if a husband, deserted his wife or children, or without just cause failed to support them for 6 months or more during the 15 years immedi-

ately preceding; if a wife, has not deserted her husband or children under 15 years of age.

7. Has not within 1 year been an habitual vagrant or beggar.

8. Has no child or other person liable for his support and able to support him.

9. Is not an inmate of and receiving the necessities of life from a public or private charitable or fraternal institution or home for the aged.

10. Does not have property in excess of $3,000.

11. Has not deprived himself of property in order to qualify for the old age pension.

Grant.—The amount of the aid is to be fixed with due regard to the conditions in each case but may not with all other income, including income from property, exceed $1 a day.

Application must be filed in writing with the county judge of the county of residence in the manner and form prescribed by the Board of County Commissioners. All statements are to be sworn to or affirmed as true. No docket fee is required for filing.

Instalments are payable monthly or quarterly according to the decision of the county judge. The amount of the aid is subject to change with change in the applicant's circumstances. Excess pensions or all pensions paid are recoverable from the estate of the pensioner and returnable to the county treasury. It is within the power of the county judge who issues the pension certificate to modify, revoke, or suspend the certificate for cause. If a pensioner violates some provision of the law governing the grant, his pension shall be canceled by the county judge. No pension is to be paid to a person while imprisoned for a crime punishable by a sentence of 1 month or longer.

No relief is to be given a pensioner from other public sources except for medical or surgical assistance. If the pensioner is incompetent to care for himself or his property, the county judge may on the testimony of three reputable witnesses as to this incompetency, pay the amount of the pension to any responsible person for the use of the pensioner.

Funeral expenses not to exceed $100 may be paid from the pension fund if the deceased person's estate is inadequate to pay them.

Transfer of property to the Board of County Commissioners to be managed for the applicant's benefit may be required by the county judge as a condition for the grant of the pension.

Pensions granted are inalienable in any form.

Penalties and offenses.—Any person who by wilfully false statement or representation, by impersonation, or other fraudulent means, obtains or helps another to obtain a pension certificate to which he is not entitled, a larger pension grant, or payment of suspended or forfeited instalments, or who aids or abets in buying or disposing of the property of a pensioner without the county judge's consent is guilty of a misdemeanor punishable by imprisonment in the county jail for not over 1 year, by a fine of not over $500 or by both fine and imprisonment. The penalty for violation of any provision of this act is similar. A pensioner convicted of an offense under this act shall have his certificate canceled.

Reports.—Not later than 30 days after the close of the calendar year, the Board of County Commissioners shall make report to the secretary of state for the year showing the amount paid by the county for pensions, the total number of applications, the number of pensions granted, the number denied, and the number canceled and such other information as the secretary of state may request.

Source of funds.—The Board of County Commissioners of each county which establishes an old age pension system shall appropriate annually sufficient money for the operation of the plan in the county. Upon order of the county judge the county treasurer shall pay the amounts ordered paid as pensions.

KENTUCKY

ACTS OF 1926, CHAP. 187

An act providing for the protection and assistance of aged needy persons in the commonwealth of Kentucky and allowing the counties to adopt the provisions of this act. Approved March 25, 1926.

The fiscal court or the county commissioners may, after first adopting the provisions of the act, establish a system of old age pensions in accordance with the provisions herein and may levy, collect, and disburse such sums of money from the general funds of their county as may be necessary to comply with the provisions of this act. After having operated under such system for one year or more, any county may abandon the system.

Administration.—The fiscal court or the county commissioners prescribe the manner and form in which application for the pension shall be made. The county judge investigates, decides upon the application, fixes the amount of the pension, and issues the pension certificate.

Qualifications of claimants.—Any person while residing in a county which maintains a system of old age pensions who complies with the provisions of this act shall be entitled to a pension in old age. An old age pension may be granted only to an applicant who—

1. Has reached seventy years of age or over.
2. Has been a United States citizen for at least 15 years before applying.
3. Has resided in the state and in the county in which he applies for at least 10 years immediately preceding.

No person shall be entitled to a pension who—

4. Is a professional beggar.
5. Can earn $400 per year.
6. Receives a pension from any source which added to his earnings makes a sum exceeding $400.

7. Possesses property to the value of $2,500 or more or who has income from any source in excess of $400 per year.

8. Is an inmate of any state, county, or charitable institution in Kentucky or elsewhere.

9. Has deprived himself of property for the purpose of qualifying for a pension.

10. Has a child or other person liable for his support and able to support him.

Grant.—The amount of the grant shall be fixed by the county judge with due regard to the conditions in each case, but in no case shall it exceed $250 per annum.

Application is to be filed in writing with the county judge of the county of residence of the applicant in the manner and form prescribed by the fiscal court or county commissioners. A rejected applicant may not re-apply for a year.

The total amount paid out in pension shall be recoverable upon death of a pensioner from any estate which he leaves and be paid into the treasury of the county which paid the pension to become a part of the old age pension fund of the county.

Penalties and offenses.—Any person who by wilfully false statement or impersonation or other fraudulent device obtains or helps another to obtain a pension to which he is not entitled shall be guilty of a misdemeanor punishable by a fine of not more than $500 or by imprisonment in the county jail for not more than one year or by both fine and imprisonment.

Source of funds.—The fiscal court or county commissioners of any county adopting this plan may levy, collect, and disburse such sums of money from the general funds of their county as may be necessary to comply with the provisions of this act.

MARYLAND

LAWS OF MARYLAND, 1927, CHAP. 538

An act establishing an old age pension system which may be adopted by Baltimore city or by counties desiring the same. Approved April 26, 1927. In effect June 1, 1927.

The mayor and council of the city of Baltimore, or the county commissioners of any county, are hereby authorized to establish a system of old age pensions in accordance with the provisions of this act. After having operated such system for one year or more, the city or county may abandon the system.

Administration.—The Board of State Aid and Charities shall from time to time prescribe and promulgate rules and regulations to carry out the provisions of this Article efficiently and shall publish such information as it may deem advisable to acquaint aged persons and the public generally with the old age pension plan of this state. The county commissioners or the supervisors of city charities of Baltimore are to prescribe the form and manner in which the appli-

cation for a pension is to be made. The judge of the circuit court for the county
or the judge of the superior court of Baltimore receives the applications when
filed, makes investigation, decides upon the application, and settles upon the
amount of the pension. His decision is to be final.

Qualifications of claimants.—Any person while residing in a county or in
Baltimore which maintains a system of old age pensions who complies with the
provisions of this Article shall be entitled to a pension in old age. The old age
pension may be granted only to a person who—

1. Has reached sixty-five years of age or over.

2. Has been a citizen of the United States for at least 15 years before making
application.

3. Has resided in the state and in the county or the city in which he makes
application for at least 15 years continuously immediately preceding application, or for 40 years at least 5 of which immediately precede application.

4. Is not at application an inmate of any prison, jail, workhouse, infirmary,
insane asylum, or other public correctional institution.

5. Has not during 10 years immediately preceding application been imprisoned for felony.

6. Has not without just cause failed to support his wife and children under
sixteen for 6 months or more during 15 years preceding the date of application
for pension.

7. Has not within 1 year preceding been an habitual tramp or beggar.

8. Has no child or other person responsible under the law of this state for his
support and able to support him.

No old age pension shall be granted or paid to a person:

9. While he is an inmate of and receives the necessities of life from any charitable institution maintained by the state or its subdivisions or from a private
charitable institution or home for the aged.

10. If the value of his property exceeds $3,000.

11. Who has deprived himself of property for the purpose of qualifying for
old age relief.

Grant.—The amount of the grant is to be fixed with due regard to the conditions of each case, but in no instance shall it be an amount which when added
to the income of the applicant from other sources including property exceeds $1
a day. Payment is monthly or quarterly.

Application for a pension must be filed in writing with the judge of the circuit court for the county or the superior court for Baltimore in the form and
manner prescribed by the county commissioners or the supervisors of city charities. All statements must be under affidavit. A rejected applicant may not
reapply until a year has elapsed.

Each pensioner shall file with the judge such reports as the county commissioners or the supervisors of the city charities of Baltimore may request. Any
pension paid in excess of the amount due in view of the resources of the pen-

sioner shall be returned to the county or city and is recoverable as a debt due. If a pensioner is convicted of any offense punishable by imprisonment for a month or longer, payments of his pension shall cease during the period of imprisonment.

Funeral expenses upon death of a pensioner shall be paid to such persons as the judge may direct. They may not exceed $125, however, and cannot be met from the deceased's estate.

No other relief shall be given by the state or its subdivisions to a pensioner while the pension continues, with the exception of medical or surgical assistance. If the pensioner is incapable of selfcare or care of the money granted, the judge may direct the pension instalments to be paid to any responsible person or corporation for benefit of the aged person or he may suspend all payment for whatever period he sees fit.

Transfer of property: If the judge deems it necessary he may require as a condition to a grant of a pension certificate that the property of the applicant be transferred to the county commissioners or the supervisors of city charities in Baltimore to be managed by them for the benefit of the applicant.

Pensions shall be inalienable in any form.

Penalties and offenses.—Wilfully false statement in obtaining a pension or helping another to get one to which he is not entitled or a larger allowance than is permissible, or a forfeited instalment grant is considered a misdemeanor and is punishable by a fine of not more than $500 or by imprisonment for not longer than a year or by both fine and imprisonment. Any violation of the provisions of this act is punishable in similar fashion. A pensioner guilty of offense of this nature upon conviction may have his certificate canceled by the judge if the judge sees fit.

Reports.—Within 30 days after the close of each calendar year, the clerk of the circuit court for each county and the clerk of the superior court for the city of Baltimore shall make report for the preceding year to the Board of State Aid and Charities, stating the amount paid for pensions, the total number of applications, the number granted, the number refused, the number canceled during the year, and such other information as the Board may deem advisable.

Source of funds.—The county commissioners of each county or the mayor and the City Council of Baltimore which establishes an old age pension system shall annually appropriate a sum of money sufficient to carry out the provisions of this act.

MASSACHUSETTS

GENERAL LAWS, CHAP. 118A

An act providing for adequate assistance to certain aged citizens and for a report by the commissioner of corporations and taxation as to ways and means for raising the required revenue. Approved May 28, 1930. To become operative July 1, 1931.

No person receiving assistance under this act shall be deemed a pauper by reason thereof.

Administration.—The department of public welfare shall supervise the work done and the measures taken by the boards of public welfare of the towns, and may make such rules relating to the administration as it deems necessary. Each board of public welfare shall, for the purpose of granting adequate assistance and service to aged persons, establish a division to be designated the Bureau of Old Age Assistance.

Such assistance shall, wherever practicable, be given to the aged person in his own home, or in lodgings, or in a boarding home, and it shall be sufficient to provide suitable and dignified care.

Qualifications of claimants.—Adequate assistance shall be granted to deserving citizens in need of relief and support, seventy years of age or over who have resided in the commonwealth not less than 20 years immediately preceding their arrival at that age, subject to such reasonable exceptions as to continuity of residence as the department of public welfare may determine. In determining the need for financial assistance, the Bureaus of Old Age Assistance shall give consideration to the resources of the aged person and to the ability of children and others to support.

Grant.—No specific amount is stated, but the assistance is to be adequate and take into consideration the aged person's needs and resources, and be given so as to provide suitable and dignified care.

Separate records are to be kept of all aged persons aided. The department of public welfare is to have access to all records and other data kept by the boards of public welfare relating to such assistance. It may require the production of books and papers and the testimony of witnesses under oath.

Source of funds.—The town rendering the assistance shall, subject to the approval of the department, be reimbursed by the commonwealth for one-third of the amount of the assistance given, or if the person so aided has no settlement in the commonwealth, for the total amount thereof.

The commissioner of corporations and taxation is hereby directed to consider ways and means for raising the revenue required by the commonwealth and by the cities and towns to carry out the terms of this act from sources which, so far as may be, will not constitute an additional burden on real estate, and shall especially consider some form of taxation on amusements, proprietary articles, and luxuries. He shall report his findings and recommendations to the general court, together with drafts of legislation necessary to carry those recommendations into effect, by filing the same with the clerk of the house of representatives not later than the first Wednesday in December of 1930.

MINNESOTA

SESSION LAWS, 1929, CHAP. 47-S.F., NO. 102.

An act relating to old age pensions. Approved and in effect March 1, 1929.

Counties may establish old age pensions through a resolution submitting the proposition to the voters which has been adopted by a majority vote of the county board. If a majority voting at the ensuing election favor the proposition so submitted, it shall be established in the county pursuant to the conditions of this act. After a trial of at least a year, it may be abandoned if a majority of the county board so votes.

Administration.—The county board shall make the rules for the administration of this act and publish such information as it may deem advisable in order to acquaint aged persons and the public generally with the old age pension plan of this state.

The district judge holds hearings, investigates, decides upon applications fixes the amount of the pension and issues the certificate. His decisions are final.

Qualifications of claimants.—Any person while residing in a county which maintains a system of old age pensions who complies with the provisions of this act is entitled to pension. The old age pension may be granted only to a person who—

1. Is seventy years old or over.

2. Has been a citizen of the United States for at least 15 years before application.

3. Has resided in the state and in the county in which he makes application continuously for at least 15 years immediately preceding application or for 40 years at least 5 of which immediately precede the application.

4. Is not an inmate of any prison, jail, workhouse, infirmary, insane asylum, or any other public correctional institution.

5. Has not during the 10 years immediately preceding been imprisoned for felony.

6. Has not, if a husband, without just cause failed to support wife and children under fifteen for 6 months or more during the 15 years preceding application.

7. Has not within 1 year preceding been an habitual tramp or beggar.

8. Has no child or other person liable for his support and able to support him.

No old age pension shall be granted or paid to a person:

9. Who is an inmate receiving the necessaries of life from any charitable institution, public or private, or home for the aged.

10. If the value of his property or the combined property of a husband and wife living together exceeds $3,000.

11. Who has deprived himself of property for the purpose of qualifying for old age relief.

Grant.—The amount of the grant shall be fixed with due regard to the conditions in each case, but in no case shall it when added to the income of the applicant (income from property included) exceed $1 a day. Payment shall be made monthly or quarterly as the district judge may decide.

Application shall be filed in writing with the district judge of the county of residence in the manner and form prescribed by the county attorney. All state-merits on it shall be sworn to or affirmed. A rejected applicant may not reapply within a year.

Each pensioner shall file with the district judge such reports as he may require. The judge may revoke or modify the pension certificate with change in the pensioner's circumstances. Excess pensions paid or all pensions paid are recoverable from the estate of the pensioned and, if obtained, are to be returned to the treasury of the county, town, city, or village which paid them out.

Funeral expenses such as the district judge may direct not to exceed $100 may be paid if the deceased's estate cannot meet them.

No other aid from the state or any of its subdivisions is to be paid a pensioner during the continuance of his pension, medical and surgical assistance excepted. If on the testimony of at least three reputable witnesses the pensioned person is found incapable, the judge may direct payment of the pension to any responsible person or corporation for the aged person's benefit, or he may suspend payment.

Transfer of property to the county may be required by the district judge as a condition for the receipt of a pension, to be managed by the county board for the pensioner's benefit.

Pensions shall be inalienable in any form.

Forfeiture of a pension may result from obtaining it by wilfully false statement or by violation of any of the provisions laid down for its granting. The pension shall cease if the pensioner is convicted of any offense punishable by imprisonment for a month or longer for the period of imprisonment.

Penalties and offenses.—Wilfully false statement in obtaining a pension or aiding another to get one to which he is not entitled, or a larger allowance than is permissible, or a forfeited instalment is considered a misdemeanor and is punishable by a fine of not over $500 or by imprisonment of not over a year, or by both fine and imprisonment. Violation of any of the provisions of this act is a misdemeanor.

Reports.—Within 30 days after the close of the calendar year, the county auditor shall make report for the preceding year to the board of county commissioners, stating the amount paid for pensions, and to whom and in what amount paid, the total number of applications, the name of each applicant, the number granted, the number denied, the number canceled, and such other information as the board may deem advisable.

Source of funds.—The county board is to provide funds and appropriate a sufficient sum annually.

Each city, town, or village shall reimburse the county for all amounts paid out to its residents of at least 5 years. The county board at its annual meeting on the county auditor's report shall fix the amount to be paid by city, town, or village. Each city, town, or village shall levy annually a tax sufficient to meet this cost. This is applicable only where the county system of caring for the poor does not obtain.

MONTANA

SESSION LAWS, 1923, CHAP. 72

An act to be hereafter named and cited as the Old Age Pension Act. Approved and in effect March 5, 1923.

Administration.—There shall be established in each county of the state of Montana a County Old Age Pension Board called the Old Age Pension Commission. Boards of County Commissioners are hereby designated the Old Age Pension Commissions of their respective counties to serve as such without any extra compensation. The procedure under this act shall be regulated in accordance with the rules and regulations laid down by the Old Age Pension Commissions from time to time.

The duties of the Old Age Pension Commissions are to make rules and regulations for the administration of this act and to meet at such times and places as it stipulates for meetings. The Commission shall receive applications in the form which it prescribes, determine the amount of pensions, and issue pension certificates.

Qualifications of claimants.—Every person shall, in the discretion of the Old Age Pension Commission, while residing in Montana be entitled to a pension in old age subject to the restrictions and qualifications noted. An old age pension may be granted only to an applicant who—

1. Has reached the age of seventy or upwards.

2. Is a citizen of the United States for at least 15 years preceding application.

3. Resides in Montana and has so resided continuously for at least 15 years immediately preceding or for 25 years at least 5 of them immediately preceding application.

4. Has not during the 10 years preceding application been imprisoned for any offense punishable by imprisonment in the state penitentiary.

5. Has not, if a husband, during the 15 years immediately preceding application for a period of 6 months or upward deserted his wife or without just cause failed to provide her with adequate means of maintenance and provide for his children under fifteen; or, if a wife, has not deserted her husband or children under age without cause.

6. Has not within 1 year preceding been a professional tramp or beggar.

7. His income from all sources does not exceed $300 per year.

8. Has not deprived himself of property for the sake of qualifying for the pension.

9. Has no child or other person legally responsible for his support and able to support him.

Grant.—The amount of the pension shall be fixed by the Old Age Pension Commission with due regard to the conditions of each case; but in no case shall it exceed $25 per month. It shall begin upon the date given in the certificate issued by the county treasurer to the claimant and be paid in monthly payments by county warrants drawn by the county treasurer upon the poor fund.

Application shall be delivered in writing by the claimant to the Old Age

Pension Commission on the form by it prescribed. All statements are to be sworn to as correct and true. It shall be the duty of the person pensioned to notify the Commission of any change in circumstances which may necessitate a change in the amount of the pension. Recovery of double the amount of the pension is allowed from the estate of a pensioned person who has received a larger pension than that to which he was entitled. Amounts so recovered are to be put in the county treasury. At death of a pensioner the total amount of pensions paid him may be allowed as a preferred claim against any estate which he leaves, amounts so gained to be put into the county treasury to the credit of the poor fund.

Funeral expenses to the amount of $100, inclusive of the instalment of the pension then accruing, may be paid by the Commission if the estate of the pensioner is not able to defray burial costs.

No other relief shall be paid during the continuance of the pension by the state or any of its subdivisions except for medical or surgical assistance.

Alienation of the pension is forbidden.

Suspension of the pension is possible if at any time the Commission has reason to think it has been improperly obtained or is for an amount larger than is permissible. If at any time the pensioner is convicted of an offense punishable by imprisonment for one month or longer, the pension shall be suspended for the term of imprisonment. If a person is found on the testimony of reputable witnesses to be incapable, the pension may be suspended or the Commission may direct that it be paid to some reputable person for the benefit of the aged person entitled to it. If the recipient of a pension is guilty of an offense against the provisions of this act he may forfeit his pension certificate. He may not apply for a new certificate until a year after the old was forfeited.

Transfer of property may be demanded by the Old Age Pension Commission as a requirement for the granting of a pension.

Penalties and offenses.—Any person who by means of wilfully false statement or representation, by impersonation or other fraudulent device obtains, or attempts to get, or aids or abets another to get an old age pension certificate to which he is not entitled, to obtain payment of a forfeited instalment, or aids in the buying or disposing of the property of a pensioner without the consent of the Old Age Pension Commission shall be guilty of a misdemeanor punishable by a fine of not over $500 or by imprisonment not to exceed 6 months or by both. The same penalty attaches to the violation of any provision of this act.

Reports.—Within 90 days of the close of the calendar year, the Old Age Pension Commission shall make a report for the preceding year to the state auditor stating the total number of recipients, the amount paid in cash, the number of applications, the number of pensions granted, the number denied, the number canceled during the year, and such other information as the state auditor may deem advisable.

Source of funds.—Funds for pensions are to be furnished by the respective counties and for all expenses of administration also. They are to be paid from the poor fund of the county by the county treasurer.

NEVADA

STATUTES OF THE STATE OF NEVADA PASSED AT THE 32D SESSION
OF THE LEGISLATURE, 1925, CHAP. 14; CHAP. 121

An act providing old age pensions, establishing uniform regulations for the benefit of the respective counties in the state of Nevada, prescribing and authorizing provision to be made by the respective counties for certain inhabitants who by reason of age or otherwise have a claim for aid from society. Approved March 18, 1925.

Construction.—This act shall be considered an act additional to all acts respecting poor persons and particularly an act entitled "An act for the support of the poor" approved November 29, 1861, and shall be construed as an exercise of power by the legislature in recognition of the just claims of the inhabitants mentioned upon the aid of society, without thereby annexing the stigma of pauperism by legal definition.

Administration.—The Board of County Commissioners (the Board) shall have authority to make such reasonable rules and regulations as may be necessary to carry out the provisions of this act. Applications are to be filed with the clerk of the Board, the Board is to set a time for a hearing of the applicant before the Board. The Board shall make its investigation, hold the hearing, and either grant or reject the application within 60 days of the filing of the application.

An appeal may be taken from the action of the Board to the district court by the applicant or by any tax-paying citizen.

Qualifications of claimants.—Subject to the provisions of this act every person while residing in the state of Nevada shall be entitled to a pension in old age. An old age pension may be granted only to a person who—

1. Has attained the age of sixty-five years or over.

2. Has been a United States citizen 15 years before application, and resided actually for 10 years preceding application in Nevada.

3. Is not at time of applying an inmate of any prison, jail, workhouse, insane asylum, or any other public reform or correctional institution.

4. Has not, if husband, for 6 months or more during the 10 years preceding the date of application for relief, deserted wife or without just cause failed to support her and his children under fifteen; or, if wife, has not deserted her husband or without just cause failed to support such of her children as were under age and she was bound to support.

5. Has not within a year preceding application been a professional tramp or beggar.

6. Has no child or other person responsible under law for his support and found by the Board able to support him.

A pension may not be granted a person who—

7. Has property the value of which exceeds $3,000.

8. Has deprived himself of property for the purpose of qualifying for old age relief.

If a pensioner is an inmate of an institution the pension is to go to the institution, to be applied towards defraying the cost of his care in it. The Board must approve the institution and have the right freely to visit it and to inspect it. Any money remaining after the cost of care has been met shall go to the person on pension. It shall not be lawful for any charitable institution receiving public money to refuse admission or relief on the ground that a person is a pensioner under this act.

Grant.—The amount of aid shall be fixed with due regard to the conditions of each case, but in no case shall it exceed $1 a day when added to the income of the applicant from all sources including property. Payment shall be monthly or quarterly as the Board shall decide.

Application shall be filed with the clerk of the board of county commissioners and all statements in it made under oath. At the hearing the applicant shall either appear in person or by attorney and present witnesses and other evidence such as is material to the application. The person pensioned must report to the Board any change in his income which may necessitate a corresponding change in the amount of his pension. Excess pensions paid are recoverable from the estate of the pensioner, and when so recovered are to be put into the old age pension fund of the county.

A certificate improperly obtained is void.

The estate of a deceased pensioner is liable for the total amount of pensions which have been paid him and the money so obtained is to go into the county treasury to the credit of the old age pension fund.

Funeral expenses may be paid by the Board to the amount of $100 if the estate cannot cover them.

No relief from the state or any of its subdivisions is allowable during the continuance of the pension except for medical or surgical assistance. When a pensioner is adjudged incompetent on the testimony of at least three reputable witnesses, the Board may direct the payment of his pension to any responsible person or corporation or suspend its payment. If paid at all it is to be used for the benefit of the aged person.

Suspension of the pension takes place for the period of detention in jail or prison for conviction of a crime punishable by imprisonment for 1 month or longer. The pension is forfeited if the person violates any of the provisions governing the granting of it.

Transfer of property may be made a condition for the granting of the pension if the Board sees fit. If transferred, the property is to be managed by the Board for the benefit of the pensioner.

Pensions shall be absolutely inalienable.

Penalties and offenses.—Obtaining a certificate fraudulently, securing a larger grant than is permissible, procuring the payment of a forfeited instalment, or aiding and abetting in the buying or selling of a pensioner's property without the consent of the Board is a misdemeanor punishable by a fine of not over

$500 or by imprisonment for not more than 1 year or by both fine and imprisonment.

Reports.—Within 30 days after the close of the calendar year, the board of county commissioners of each county of the state shall report through its clerk to the governor covering fully the administration and operation of the act for the preceding year. The report shall state the total number of pensions, the total cash paid in pensions and in administration, separately, the number of applications in the year, the number granted, the number denied, the number canceled and such other information as the governor may request.

Source of funds.—The county commissioners and all officers having to do with the assessment of property and the collection of taxes in each of the counties of the state may and are hereby empowered and authorized to provide funds in an amount sufficient to carry out the provisions and regulations of this act.

NEW YORK

LAWS OF NEW YORK, 1930, CHAP. 387

An act to amend the public welfare law, in relation to providing security against old age want. Approved April 10, 1930. In effect May 1, 1930. Relief under this law not to begin before January 1, 1931.

Declaration of object, application, and effect.—The care and relief of aged persons who are in need and whose physical or other condition or disability seems to render permanent their inability to provide properly for themselves is hereby declared to be a special matter of state concern and a necessity in promoting the public health and welfare. To provide such care and relief at public expense, a state-wide system of old age relief is hereby established, to operate in a uniform manner with due regard to the varying living conditions and costs of living. . . . . Other provisions of this chapter not inconsistent with this article shall be applied and used in carrying out the provisions of this article. Provisions of any city charter or other local or special act forbidding outdoor relief, or which are inconsistent with the provisions of this article, shall not apply to the relief provided by this article, nor impair nor limit the state-wide operation of this article, according to its terms. The term "relief" whenever used in this article shall be construed to include assistance, aid, care, or support.

Administration.—As provided in this article, old age relief shall be given by city and county public welfare districts and by such other cities as may elect to administer old age relief, subject to partial reimbursement by the state and to supervision by the state department of social welfare. If the public welfare official does not take action upon an application within 30 days, or denies the applicant, appeal may be made to the state department and it will review the case. Its decision will be binding upon the public welfare official.

Complaints relative to the manner of administration of old age relief may be filed in writing with the state department which will investigate, decide, and notify the public welfare official of its findings and whether it will approve further payments, and in what amounts.

Qualifications of claimants.—Old age relief is to be given to any person who—

1. Has attained the age of seventy years.
2. Is unable to support himself in whole or in part and has no child or other person able and responsible for his support.
3. Is a citizen of the United States.
4. Has been a resident of the state of New York for at least 10 years immediately preceding his application for old age relief.
5. Has resided in and been an inhabitant of the public welfare district in which the application is made for at least 1 year immediately preceding application.
6. Is not at the time an inmate of any public or private home for the aged, or any public home, or any public or private institution of a custodial, correctional, or curative character, except in the case of temporary medical or surgical care in a hospital.
7. Has not made a voluntary assignment or transfer of property for the purpose of qualifying for relief.
8. Is not because of his physical or mental condition in need of continued institutional care.

Grant.—The amount and nature of the relief and the manner of providing it shall be determined by the public welfare official with due regard to the conditions of each case, in accordance with the rules and regulations of the state department. Relief may include, among other things, medical and surgical care and nursing. Whenever practicable relief may be granted in the form of cash or a check. Whenever practicable, too, it shall be provided for the recipient in his own or some other suitable family home. It shall be the duty of public welfare officials to provide adequately for those eligible to this relief.

Application shall be made by the person to the public welfare official of the public welfare district in which he resides. An inmate of an institution may make application while still an inmate, but the relief will not become payable as long as he remains in the institution. The application may be made in person or through another and in writing or reduced to writing. It must specify that it is for relief under this article.

Revocation or reduction of the amount of relief is possible for cause as is also suspension of payments. Periodic reconsideration of each case is required.

Relief is not assignable and is inalienable.

Penalties and offenses.—Any person, who by means of a false statement or representation, or by impersonation or other fraudulent device, obtains or attempts to obtain, or aids or abets any person to obtain old age relief to which he is not entitled, or a larger amount of relief, shall be guilty of a misdemeanor, unless such act constitutes a violation of the penal law of New York in which case he shall be punished in accordance with the penalties fixed by such law.

Reports.—Each public welfare official shall report to the state department at such times and in such manner and form as the department may prescribe, the number of applications granted, the grants of relief changed, revoked, or suspended by him, together with copies of all applications and supporting affidavits received and statement of the official acting thereon, and the amount of the relief to aged paid out by the public welfare district under this article, and make such other reports as the state department may require.

Source of funds.—Subject to partial reimbursement by the state, each public welfare district shall furnish the old age relief provided here to persons eligible who reside in its territory. A city may by majority vote of its legislative body elect to furnish such old age relief to its inhabitants, in which case the city shall have all powers and duties relative to old age relief conferred by this article upon a public welfare district, and be entitled to partial reimbursement by the state as is the district.

County or city money is to be provided by appropriation of its legislative body. The state shall reimburse the public welfare district or city to the extent of one-half its expenditures for relief for each aged person and one-half the administrative expenses. Claims for reimbursement are to be presented by the respective public welfare districts semiannually in January and July.

Saving clause.—A person seventy years of age or over not receiving old age relief under this article is not by reason of his age debarred from receiving public relief and care under other provisions of this chapter.

PENNSYLVANIA

LAWS OF PENNSYLVANIA, SESSION OF 1923, NO. 141

An act providing for and regulating, subject to certain restrictions, limitations, and liabilities, assistance to certain aged persons and providing for their burial, etc. Approved May 10, 1923.

Administration.—An Old Age Assistance Commission is created which shall be composed of three citizens of the commonwealth, appointed by the governor, for a term of 4 years. The Commission shall appoint an old age assistance superintendent qualified by character, training, and experience who, with the approval of the Commission, shall appoint the necessary number of assistants and fix their duties and salaries. The Commission shall make the rules and regulations for the carrying out of the provisions of this act. In each county there shall be established a county old age assistance board, consisting of three persons domiciled in the county, who shall be appointed by the county commissioners for a term of 4 years and serve without pay, except necessary expenses. The Board may appoint one or more local investigators at a salary of not over $900 per year. The Commission and the Board shall meet at such times and places as the Commission may set. The Board of the county of residence shall receive and pass upon applications, in the manner and form prescribed by the Commission. The Board shall investigate each application and send a copy of the application and of its decision thereon to the Commission. The Commission may make such further investigation as it desires through the superintendent or the Board and may direct a rehearing before the Board. The Commission shall decide upon the application and fix the amount of the pension and its decision shall be final.

Qualifications of claimants.—Every person while resident in the commonwealth shall be entitled to assistance in old age subject to the provisions and restrictions of this act. Assistance may be granted to a person who—

1. Is seventy years of age or over.

2. Has been a citizen of the United States for at least 15 years preceding application.

3. Resides in the commonwealth and has so resided continuously for at least 15 years immediately preceding application, or for 40 years at least 5 of which immediately precede application.

4. Is not an inmate of any prison, jail, workhouse, insane asylum, or any other public reform or correctional institution.

5. Has not, if a husband, for 6 months or more during the 15 years preceding application deserted his wife or without just cause failed to support her and his children under fifteen; if a wife, has not deserted her husband or failed to support such of her children as were under age and she was bound to support.

6. Has not within 1 year preceding been a professional tramp or beggar.

7. Has no child or other person responsible for his support and able to support him, as found out by the Board or Commission.

An old age pension shall not be granted to a person who—

1. Has property the value of which exceeds $3,000.

2. Disposes of property in order to qualify for old age assistance.

Grant.—The amount is to be fixed with due regard to the conditions of each case, but not to exceed $1 a day when added to the applicant's income from all other sources.

Application is to be made in writing to the Board of the county of residence in the manner and form prescribed by the Commission. All statements are to be sworn to or affirmed. If an applicant is rejected he may not re-apply within a year. It is the duty of the pensioned person to notify the Board of any increase in the amount of his income so that the pension grant may be adjusted or canceled if not needed. Any excess pension paid is recoverable from the person as a debt due the commonwealth. The amount of all pensions paid is deductible at death from the pensioner's estate and payable into the treasury of the commonwealth. Recovery of double the amount of assistance in excess of that to which the recipient was entitled is possible as a preferred claim against the estate also.

The amount of the assistance shall be paid to the governing authorities of any charitable or benevolent or fraternal institution of which the person receiving assistance is an inmate, and applied toward defraying the expenses of such person in the institution, provided that the Commission has given approval and is permitted freely to visit the institution and inspect it. Any balance above cost of care is to go to the person pensioned. The recipient of old age assistance is not to be refused admission or relief by a charitable institution.

No other relief from the commonwealth or its subdivisions is to be given a recipient of old age assistance except for medical or surgical assistance. If the recipient is adjudged incapable of using the assistance wisely, the grant may be paid to some other responsible person for the aged person's benefit.

Assistance under this act is to be inalienable.

Funeral expenses to the amount of $100 will be allowed if the deceased's estate cannot meet them.

Transfer of property may be required as a condition for the granting of assistance.

Suspension of a certificate pending inquiry into whether the certificate has been improperly obtained is provided for. If a person on pension is imprisoned for an offense punishable by imprisonment for at least 1 month, the assistance is not to be paid for the term of imprisonment. If an assisted person violates any of the provisions for obtaining the grant, it may serve as cause for cancellation of the assistance.

Penalties and offenses.—Obtaining assistance through fraud or misrepresentation or aiding another to obtain such assistance is a misdemeanor and punishable by a fine not to exceed $500 or by imprisonment not to exceed 1 year or by both fine and imprisonment. The same penalty holds for the violation of the provisions upon which these grants are made.

Reports.—The Commission is to make report within 90 days of the end of the calendar year stating the total number of recipients, the amount paid in cash, the number of applications, number granted, denied, and canceled, and such other information as the Commission may desire.

Source of funds.—All expenses of the county boards in administration, investigation, and salaries are to be paid by the county treasurer from county money. Payment of assistance, expenses, etc., of the Commission are to be paid by the state treasurer out of money specifically appropriated for the purpose upon orders of the superintendent and warrant of the auditor general.

[NOTE.—In 1924, this law was declared unconstitutional, largely on the basis of a clause in the state constitution which prohibits the legislature from making appropriations for charitable, educational, and benevolent purposes.]

UTAH

LAWS OF UTAH, 1929, CHAP. 76, H.B. NO. 28

The Old Age Pension Law of the State of Utah, an act relating to the support of the poor and infirm, providing for old age pensions. Approved March 25, 1929. In effect May 14, 1929.

This is to constitute an additional method for the support of the poor of a county.

Administration.—Power to grant the pension is in the hands of the county commissioners called the Board, as a part of their other powers and duties in relation to the support of the poor.

Qualifications of claimants.—The pension may be granted to any person who—

1. Has reached sixty-five and is incapacitated to learn a livelihood.

2. Is and has been for the 15 years last past a citizen of the United States.

3. Is and has been for the 15 years last past a resident of Utah or a resident of the state for 25 years, the last 5 of which have been continuous.

4. Is and for 5 years immediately preceding application has been an actual bona fide resident of the county.

5. Has not in last 10 years been imprisoned for a felony or indictable misdemeanor.

6. Has not, if a husband, in the 10 years last past deserted or without just cause failed to provide adequate means of support for wife and children under fifteen for a period of at least 6 months; and, if a wife, has not deserted husband and children under fifteen in the last 15 years without cause.

7. Has not within 1 year last past been vagrant or a beggar.

8. Has not during the year last past had an income exceeding $300.

9. Has not deprived himself of property for the purpose of qualifying.

10. Has no relative responsible under the law for his support who is able to support him.

Grant.—The amount of the monthly pension shall be determined by the Board but shall not exceed $25. The recipient shall notify the Board of change in his circumstances and the amount of his pension may be varied to take account of increased income.

Application shall be in writing upon blanks furnished by the county auditor and signed and verified under oath by the applicant and supported by the affidavits of two reputable citizens of the county. The application must cover all the information needed in order to determine eligibility to the pension.

The Board has the right to recover by civil action from the recipient for excess pensions paid or for pensions paid because of fraudulent representations. The county also has a claim against the estate of a deceased pensioner for all pensions paid. Amounts recovered are to be paid into the county treasury.

Funeral expenses not to exceed $100 may be provided by the Board if the estate is inadequate to pay them.

No other aid is to be given a pensioner by the state or its subdivisions except for medical or surgical assistance.

Pensions are inalienable.

Suspension of the payment of the pension while imprisonment lasts shall occur if the recipient is convicted of crime and imprisoned.

If the recipient is adjudged incapable, the Board may pay the allowance to some other responsible person for his benefit.

False statement or representation disqualifies the recipient. Reapplication is not permitted within a year.

Transfer of property to the county in whole or in part may be required by the Board as a condition of the grant, as security for the repayment of the pension.

Source of funds.—The county commissioners are to provide funds. They shall have power to provide funds for the purpose of this act in relation to their other powers and duties with reference to the support of the poor.

WISCONSIN

STATUES 1925, CHAP. 49, RELIEF AND SUPPORT OF THE POOR; AMENDED, 1929, C. 181

Old Age Pensions, State Aid. For the more humane care of aged dependent persons a state system of old age assistance is hereby established. Approved May 12, 1925, to take effect on publication May 13, 1925. Approved as amended June 14, 1929. In effect on publication, June 15, 1929.

Administration.—This system of old age assistance shall be administered in each county by the county judge, under the supervision of the Board of Control. The Board of Control shall make such rules and regulations to carry out the provisions of this act efficiently as it deems advisable and acquaint aged persons and the public generally with the old age assistance plan of this state. The county judge is to make, or cause to be made, prompt investigation of all applications filed with him, decide upon applications and fix the amount of old age assistance and his decision is final.

Qualifications of claimants.—Any person who complies with the provisions set down here is entitled to financial assistance in old age. Old age assistance may be granted anyone who—

1. Is seventy years of age or over.

2. Has been a citizen of the United States at least 15 years before application.

3. Has resided in the state and in the county in which he applies for at least 15 years continuously preceding application or for 40 years at least 5 of which immediately precede application.

4. Is not at application an inmate of any prison, jail, workhouse, infirmary, insane asylum, or any other public correctional institution.

5. Has not been imprisoned in the 10 years immediately preceding for felony.

6. Has not, if a husband, failed to support wife and children under fifteen for 6 months or more during 15 years preceding date of application.

7. Has not within 1 year of application been an habitual tramp or beggar.

8. Has no child or other person responsible and able for his support.

Old age assistance shall not be granted to any person who—

9. Is an inmate receiving the necessaries of life from any charitable institution maintained by a state or its subdivisions or from any charitable, benevolent, or fraternal institution or home for the aged.

10. Has property the value of which exceeds $3,000.

11. Has deprived himself of property for the purpose of qualifying.

Grant.—The amount of the assistance shall be fixed with due regard to the conditions of each case, but in no instance shall it exceed $1 a day when added to the person's income from all other sources. Instalments shall be paid monthly or quarterly as the county judge may decide.

Application shall be filed with the county judge in the county of residence in the form and manner prescribed by the Board of Control. All statements in it are to be sworn to or affirmed. If rejected, reapplication may not be made within a year. Each person assisted shall file with the county judge such reports as the Board of Control may require. The judge may vary the amount of aid with change in the circumstances of the beneficiary. Excess assistance given is recoverable by the county as a debt due, and the entire amount of old age assistance paid is recoverable from the estate of a deceased beneficiary and when so recovered is to be put into the treasuries from which the assistance was paid out.

Funeral expenses not to exceed $100 may be paid if the estate is inadequate to meet them.

No other relief is to be given by the state or its subdivisions during the period of old age assistance with the exception of medical or surgical assistance. If in the judgment of at least three reputable witnesses the beneficiary is adjudged incompetent the assistance may be paid to another for his benefit.

The old age assistance is inalienable.

Suspension of a grant pending inquiry may be made by the county judge if he has reason to think assistance has been improperly obtained. The penalty for violation of the provisions governing the granting of the assistance by the beneficiary is cancellation of his certificate, by the county judge. If a beneficiary is convicted of a crime which carries with it a penalty of imprisonment for at least a month, the assistance is suspended for the period of imprisonment.

Transfer of property to the Board of Control may be made a condition for the grant if the county judge deems it necessary.

Penalties and offenses.—Obtaining a certificate fraudulently or by misrepresentation, securing a larger grant than that to which he is entitled or getting the payment of a forfeited instalment, is a misdemeanor, punishable by a fine of not over $500 or by imprisonment for not over 1 year or by both fine and imprisonment. Aiding and abetting another to do these is also a misdemeanor. The violation of any of the provisions of the act carries a similar penalty and for the beneficiary the cancellation of the certificate.

Reports.—Within 30 days of the close of the calendar year, a report for the preceding year is to be sent by the county clerk to the State Board of Control, stating the amount of old age assistance, the number of applications, the number granted, denied, and canceled, and such other information as the Board of Control may deem advisable.

Source of funds.—The cost of old age assistance shall in the first instance be borne by the county, but the county shall be entitled to reimbursement from the state and from cities, villages, and towns in which the beneficiaries resided. The provisions of this act regarding old age assistance apply only to counties which have made appropriations for carrying it out.

The state assists to one-third of the county's expenditures. For state aid for old age pensions on January 1, 1930, not to exceed $35,000 and annually beginning January 1, 1931, $45,000 was appropriated by the legislature, in 1929.

WYOMING

SESSION LAWS OF WYOMING, 1929, CHAP. 87

Old Age Pension Act of State of Wyoming. Approved February 19, 1929. In effect June 1, 1930.

The Act is enacted into law for the purpose of permitting the Boards of County Commissioners to handle the care and maintenance of the poor more economically and efficiently. It is recognized that under the present system the cost of maintaining the dependent poor is greatly in excess of the amount which this act proposes to allot to each, and consequently nothing in this act shall be construed as authorizing the county commissioners or the Old Age Pension Commission to pay out for old age pensions in a year an amount in excess of that represented by a levy of one-fourth mill on the total assessed value of property within the county.

Administration.—A County Old Age Pension Board is established in each county and designated the Old Age Pension Commission. The Boards of County Commissioners are these Commissions and are to serve without added compensation. The Commissions are to make the rules and regulations for carrying out the provisions of the act and to meet at such times and places as they determine.

Qualifications of claimants.—Every person shall in the discretion of the Old Age Pension Commission while resident in Wyoming be entitled to pension in old age subject to the restrictions and qualifications laid down in this act. The pension may be granted only to a person who—

1. Is sixty-five years of age or over.

2. Has been a United States citizen for at least 15 years.

3. Resides and has domicile in Wyoming and has so resided continuously for at least 15 years preceding application for the pension, and for 5 years immediately preceding in the county in which he applies.

4. Has not in the 10 years immediately preceding been imprisoned in the state penitentiary for any offense.

5. If a husband, has not deserted his spouse or without just cause failed to support her and his children under fifteen for 6 months or more during the 15 years immediately preceding application; if a wife, has not without cause deserted her husband or children under age.

6. Has not within 1 year preceding been a professional tramp or beggar.

7. Has not income from all sources in excess of $360 per annum.

8. Has not disposed of property for the purpose of qualifying for old age relief.

9. Has no child or other person legally liable for his support and able to support him.

Grant.—The amount of the old age pension is to be fixed by the Commission with due regard to the conditions of each case, but in no instance is it to exceed $30 a month. Payments are to be made monthly by county warrants drawn on the county treasurer and the poor fund of the county.

Application is to be made in writing to the Old Age Pension Commission of the county of residence. All statements in it are to be sworn to or affirmed. It is the duty of the person pensioned to notify the Commission of any increase in his income in order that the amount of the pension may be adjusted. Double the amount of relief granted in excess of that to which the recipient is entitled may be recovered by the county as a debt due and, if so recovered, is to be returned to the county treasury. Recovery of all the pensions paid a person is authorized from the estate, this amount also to go into the county treasury to the credit of the poor fund. The county from which a pensioner moves by reason of illness or for other justifiable cause shall continue his pension until he is able to qualify in the new county to which he has moved.

Funeral expenses not to exceed $100 may be paid by the Commission if the estate is unable to meet them.

No other relief from the state or any of its subdivisions is to be paid a person on pension with the exception of medical and surgical assistance.

The pension cannot be assigned or attached and is absolutely inalienable.

Suspension of the pension may take place while special inquiry is being made into the correctness of the amount of the grant in view of changed circumstances. A pension improperly obtained may be suspended or revoked. If a pensioner offends by violating some provision laid down with reference to obtaining the grant, his certificate may be cancelled and if so forfeited may not be reapplied for within a year.

Transfer of property to the Old Age Pension Commission may be demanded as a condition for the pension.

Penalties and offenses.—Obtaining a pension fraudulently is considered a misdemeanor and is punishable by a fine of not over $500 or by imprisonment for not over 6 months or by both fine and imprisonment. The penalty is the same for aiding and abetting another to obtain a pension to which he is not entitled. Violation of the provisions of the act for which no specific penalty is set is to receive similar punishment.

Reports.—Within 90 days after the close of the calendar year, the Commission is to report to the state auditor stating the total number of recipients, the number of applications, the number granted, denied, or cancelled in the year, and such other information as the state auditor may deem advisable.

Source of funds.—Funds for pensions and for all expenses of administration also shall be furnished by the counties and be paid by the county treasurer from the poor fund of the county.

INDEX

PRINTED IN U·S·A

GROWING OLD

An Arno Press Collection

Birren, James E., et al., editors. **Human Aging**. 1963

Birren, James E., editor. **Relations of Development and Aging**. 1964

Breckinridge, Elizabeth L. **Effective Use of Older Workers**. 1953

Brennan, Michael J., Philip Taft, and Mark Schupack. **The Economics of Age**. 1967

Cabot, Natalie H. **You Can't Count On Dying**. 1961

Clark, F. Le Gros. **Growing Old in a Mechanized World**. 1960

Clark, Margaret and Barbara G. Anderson. **Culture and Aging**. 1967

Crook, G[uy] H[amilton] and Martin Heinstein. **The Older Worker in Industry**. 1958

Derber, Milton, editor. **Aged and Society**. 1950

Donahue, Wilma, et al., editors. **Free Time**. 1958

Donahue, Wilma and Clark Tibbitts, editors. **New Frontiers of Aging**. 1957

Havighurst, Robert J. and Ruth Albrecht. **Older People**. 1953

International Association of Gerontology. **Old Age in the Modern World**. 1955

Kaplan, Oscar J., editor. **Mental Disorders in Later Life**. 1956

Kutner, Bernard, et al. **Five Hundred Over Sixty**. 1956

Lowenthal, Marjorie F. **Lives in Distress**. 1964

Munnichs, J.M.A. **Old Age and Finitude**. 1966

Nassau, Mabel L. **Old Age Poverty in Greenwich Village**. 1915

National Association of Social Workers. **Social Group Work with Older People**. 1963

Neugarten, Bernice L., et al. **Personality in Middle and Late Life**. 1964

Orton, Job. **Discourses to the Aged**. 1801

Pinner, Frank A., Paul Jacobs, and Philip Selznick. **Old Age and Political Behavior**. 1959

Reichard, Suzanne, Florine Livson and Paul G. Peterson. **Aging and Personality**. 1962

Rowntree, B. Seebohm. **Old People**. 1947

Rubinow, I[saac] M[ax]., editor. **Care of the Aged**. 1931

Shanas, Ethel. **The Health of Older People**. 1962

Shanas, Ethel, et al. **Old People in Three Industrial Societies**. 1968

Sheldon, J[oseph] H. **The Social Medicine of Old Age**. 1948

Shock, N[athan] W., editor. **Perspectives in Experimental Gerontology**. 1966

Tibbitts, Clark, editor. **Social Contribution by the Aging**. 1952

Tibbitts, Clark and Wilma Donahue, editors. **Social and Psychological Aspects of Aging**. 1962

U.S. Dept. of Health, Education, and Welfare. **Working With Older People**. 1970

Vischer, A[dolf] L[ucas]. **Old Age**. 1947

Welford, A[lan] T[raviss], and James E. Birren, editors. **Decision Making and Age**. 1969

Williams, Richard H., Clark Tibbitts, and Wilma Donahue, editors. **Processes of Aging**. 1963